All Downhill From Here

Our John o' Groats to Land's End Cycling Adventure, and How You Can Do It Too

PAUL WATERS

Balance Health and Fitness Limited –
www.balancehealthandfitness.co.uk

First published in Great Britain by Balance Health and Fitness Limited in
2021

ISBN 978-1-8384329-0-4

Typefaces used in this book: Book Antiqua & Century

To everyone who finds joy in adventure, seeking out new places and experiences, and making those journeys under their own steam.

Contents

Part 2: How to Have Your Own End-to-End Adventure

About This Book

The majority of this book tells the story of my own John o' Groats to Land's End cycling adventure in 2007, accompanied by my great friend Simon and our partners at the time.

I also wanted to make the book as useful as possible for those of you who might consider taking on this wonderful challenge, so Section 2 gives you a range of guidance on how to plan and enjoy your own End-to-End cycling adventure. There are admittedly plenty of insights in the main bulk of the book as well, mostly about what we learned not to do by getting it wrong. This second part is, however, broken down into specific sections. I cover topics like how to plan the route, the ever-controversial decision about whether to go south to north, or vice versa, training, nutritional advice, psychological coping mechanisms and more.

This guidance is targeted primarily towards leisure cyclists and those with less experience of taking on big adventures. If you're an experienced cyclist, or a bike geek with detailed knowledge of the inner (and outer) workings of a bicycle, you will still find there are some useful hints and tips around training, nutrition, and equipment, but I've deliberately designed it not to be too technical – so it's accessible to anybody who wants to take on this wonderful challenge. I truly believe that anyone can do it with the right planning, preparation, training, and timeframe.

The aim is that this book can be read simply as a fun tale of adventure, travel, friendship, and cycling, but also be useful if you're considering, or even planning, your own attempt. Whichever way you choose to read it, I hope you enjoy it. And if you are planning to take on the challenge, then I wish you the very best of luck.

Part 1: Our End-to-End Adventure

Chapter 1: In the Beer-ginning

'I always thought you were a bit of a ~#%*' said Simon, my best friend and partner in many cycling and exercise adventures since 2007. Cycling from John o' Groats to Land's End was our very first, and it had begun in the same way many great ideas come about – with a trip to the pub.

It was 2006 and one of the many balmy summer nights we had that year, the sort you always get in English Romcoms, except I'm not Hugh Grant and Simon certainly isn't Julia Roberts. We were out enjoying a few drinks with our partners at the time, Bek and Kirsty. Simon, Kirsty, and the rest of our friend group all lived in Clifton; the upmarket area of Bristol perched high above the city. Its name derives from the old English for, 'to mow down pedestrians in your entirely pointless 4 x 4,' or possibly, 'hillside settlement' – I'll let you decide which is correct.

I'd known Simon for around a year or so. We'd been introduced by a mutual friend when I'd moved to Bristol the previous year. That mutual friend, Alan, was also the reason why Simon thought of me as a ~#%*. You see, Alan had been in a long-term relationship with

Bek, but they had separated, and we were now together. They remained friends, and we all used to hang out together without issue. In fact, we got along famously, but Simon had hoped the two of them would get back together and saw me, the northern outsider, as the problem. I'm actually from just south of Birmingham, but Simon's Hampshire upbringing means he views anyone originating from above the M4 as a coalmining, heavy-drinking, pigeon-racing, fully-fledged northerner. Being a well-spoken southerner, brought up through the public-school system, he was very much on board with the heavy drinking aspect, but still wary of anyone with a strong regional accent.

As it turned out, all of us boys are still close friends to this day, whilst the women in this story have long since moved on – not in the next world sense, thankfully, just in the "having enough common sense to get as far away from us two Lycra-loving idiots as possible" - sense.

But I digress, let's get back to 2006. We'd been to the Hop House, the pub you could see from Kirsty and Simon's front window and, as the evening had progressed, so had we, albeit about 20 feet down the road to a tiny bar fittingly called Amoeba. It was always ram-packed, which meant three or four people had managed to squeeze inside, and tonight it was our turn.

We'd been chatting for a while and, although Simon was still wary of me – the invader from the mysterious lands of the North – we'd discovered we actually had a lot more in common than he could ever have expected. We were both ardent Liverpool fans, as was Alan. We'd both also run the London Marathon in 2005, our first attempt at the 26.2-mile distance, and we'd done so with similar motivations. Both of us had lost close friends to epilepsy and had run to raise money for related charities.

Mike had been a very good friend of mine. He was a top, top man. As well as being epileptic, he was also a type 1 diabetic and, if I'm being honest, he was never the healthiest person. He loved our nights out in Redditch town centre. We would visit the same three pubs every time (there were only three) and then make our way to the one and only nightclub. Afterwards, slightly worse for wear, we'd get a pizza from Italiano's on Unicorn Hill, then head to someone's house and talk nonsense, which mostly consisted of reciting Alan Partridge quotes, into the early hours. He was always the life and soul of the party. Tragically, one night in 2004 during the European Football Championships, he had an epileptic seizure in his sleep and died.

Before Mike's passing, my main sport had always been football. I was never interested in running a marathon. I was a full-time personal trainer, and would often run with clients, or in between sessions, but the thought of running that far just seemed utter madness, and a little pointless to be honest. All of a sudden there was a very good reason to run that far: to honour Mike's memory and to raise money for the National Society for Epilepsy. Stu, a very good friend of mine and one of Mike's closest mates, decided to take it on too. Surprisingly, I really enjoyed the hard work, the buzz of the race and the feeling of doing something in aid of a worthy cause – and that's how I got hooked on doing silly things.

Back in Bar Amoeba, Simon and I were talking about what it had been like to run the marathon, the challenges of the training and all the other things around it, like finding the balance between eating healthily and eating enough, and the difficulties in getting sponsorship (these were the days before fundraising websites and apps). We agreed that, since the marathon, our motivation had waned; we needed another challenge to inspire us.

Simon was a huge fan of cycling – the sort of fan that dons full Lycra kit just to sit and watch the Tour de France. He was into it long before it was as popular as it is now, but he didn't get out on the bike too often. I was even less prepared. I hadn't really ridden a bike properly since my teenage years. I had a nice yellow mountain bike in the garage that I'd exchanged for some PT sessions with a client, but it didn't get much action. I did, however, love a fitness challenge, and the thought of building on the London Marathon adventure, with the infamous British 'End-to-End' cycle challenge, had been in the back of my mind for some time.

There are a number of classic British fitness challenges – the aforementioned London Marathon, summiting the Three Peaks of Snowdon, Scafell and Ben Nevis inside 24 hours – the Coast-to-Coast bike ride, from the Irish Sea on the west coast to the North Sea on the east side, the fearsome Channel swim and, of course, Land's End to John o' Groats.

In the cycling community, the latter has assumed a status akin to that of a pilgrimage. Celebrated as the journey from the very bottom to the very top of Britain, it is a journey that, by road, is a minimum of 838 miles. Some dispute its top to bottom claim. Dunnet Head and various other bits of Scottish coastline are further north than John o' Groats; and Lizard Point, in Cornwall, is the most southerly tip of mainland Britain.

Geography zealots aside, 'LeJog' or, done the other way, 'JogLe', is still the cycling fanatic's route of choice. It is the longest distance you can travel by land between two points on mainland Britain unless, of course, you side with the view of the wonderfully grumpy Bill Bryson. In *The Road to Little Dribbling*, he points out that the journey is not a straight line and that, if you can zigzag, then the distance travelable is potentially much longer. He concludes that the longest straight-line journey from south to north is between Bognor Regis, in West Sussex, and the wonderfully named Cape Wrath in the Highlands. The lack of a suitable Roman road, and the amount of trespassing and carrying your bike over garden fences that would be required does, however, make this an impractical choice.

Whatever your point of view, the popularity of the Land's End to John o' Groats journey is unquestionable. I decided to look up the history of this epic journey. My internet search took me in the first instance, as is so often the case, to Wikipedia. I'll concede that the ease with which this site can be edited by anybody has led to doubts about its accuracy. There have indeed been famous instances of misuse, such as the made-up articles about the Norwegian sport of synchronised football, the mediaeval torture device known as the 'Spanish Tickler', and the unmasking of Ernest Hemingway as the true author of the *Spot the Dog* book series. And whilst I can in no way vouch for the truth or accuracy of the following claims about the history of the LeJog challenge, they sound, at the very least, quite plausible. Land's End to John o' Groats was, apparently, first walked by two brothers, John and Robert Naylor in 1871. It's not clear when it was first achieved by bike, though it is claimed that one Alfred Nixon, of the London Tricycle Club, completed his three-wheeled version of the journey in 1882. It's been run, skateboarded, ridden on horseback, done in a wheelchair, paddle-boarded, kayaked, completed on a Penny Farthing (in a ridiculously fast four and a half days), 'commuted' by bus and even 'golfed' – that is to say, in 2005, David Sullivan walked 1,100 miles end to end, hitting a golf ball all the way. How many golf balls were lost to the sea, seagulls injured, or car windscreens smashed, is not mentioned. It has even been swum. At first, I'd imagined someone snorkelling along the myriad brooks, streams, and rivers of Britain, bobbing up every now and then to check the map, but upon reading further, I discovered they had simply followed a coastal route.

The fastest recorded journey on a standard bicycle is an incredible 43 hours, 25 minutes, 13 seconds. But the overall record belongs to Andy Wilkinson, who completed it in a mind-blowing 41 hours, 4 minutes, 22 seconds on one of those crazy recumbent cycles. You know the ones, they're so low that they're impossible for any traffic to see, so they often have a flagpole on the back – not unlike what you'll find on the greens of your local golf course. I just hope he wasn't doing his attempt at the same time as golfer David Sullivan.

It must have been close to midnight in Bar Amoeba by now, and Simon was pretty merry; a combination of mild sunstroke from the heat that day, and the fact that he has far more of that 'northern spirit' for drinking than I do. In this state, it was easy to get him excited at the prospect of taking on an End-to-End charity fundraising challenge. I simply got him imagining spending days in similarly glorious weather, clad head to toe in the colourful Lycra of his favourite cycling team, focused solely on riding from one beautiful place to another.

All of this, of course, whilst being waited on hand and foot by a vast support team – a chef preparing pancakes for breakfast, with fresh orange juice and coffee; the team car always following just behind, equipped for a quick bike-swap should we suffer the misfortune of a puncture (which we wouldn't of course), a soigneur (team masseuse) ready to rub down his tired legs at the end of another hard day in the saddle, leaving him feeling fresh and able to enjoy his vin rouge from a comfy camp chair, as the sun set over the hills behind. Our partners were rightly suspicious about who exactly I had in mind to fulfil these team roles, but I knew my first job was to convince Simon and then, hopefully, the rest would follow. We shook hands on it, but I'm pretty sure – as he strolled home that warm, still night – he thought no more about it, and certainly didn't anticipate that it would actually happen.

I, however, had other ideas. The next day I was up bright and early and set about planning the route from one end of the country to the other. This basically involved opening the RAC Route Planner on my laptop, inserting John o' Groats as the start point and Land's End as the destination. I'd already convinced myself that this was the correct way to do the ride, heading south towards warmer climes and also, surely, downhill all the way. Common wisdom dictates you head south to north so as to take advantage of the prevailing winds, but I figured if we did it in summertime it wouldn't be that windy, and the improvements in weather as we headed further south would more than make up for it anyway.

Some of you may remember the RAC Route Planner, or one of the similar websites that existed as the forerunners of the Sat Nav. This was 2006, remember? The modern world was well on its way, but still needed refining and wasn't always that simple. Once you'd planned your journey, you'd simply print it out (all 27 pages of it) and attempt to follow the directions, line by line, whilst driving.

This usually led to heated debates with your passenger-come-navigator, about whether you should have taken the last left, followed by them telling you where you could stick your route planner. Worse still, if you were driving alone, it meant scrolling your finger down the page as you travelled straight over roundabout after roundabout, trying to make sure you turned left at the 86th one as instructed. Lose your place on the page, and you were hopelessly lost and might as well head home to begin the journey again, a bit like a giant game of snakes and ladders.

It wasn't the safest way of getting from A to B, and I do wonder how many people missed a vital bend in the road whilst counting back how many right turns they had made, ploughed into the roadside signage, and had to call the RAC to tow them to the nearest garage.

Maybe that was their cunning plan all along?

My first attempt at a route was largely unsuccessful, in that it appeared to direct me to a small industrial estate in Oakham, about 25 miles east of Leicester. Oakham is the county town of the Rutland, sitting not far from the eponymous and stunningly picturesque reservoir and nature reserve. The problem is, barring Rutland Water, the tiny county of Rutland is actually land-locked, so an unlikely destination to aim for in an End-to-End journey of Britain.

It appeared the route planner had decided that surely I didn't intend to travel the whole length of our fair isle on one of the most iconic routes known; what I wanted instead was to head from John o' Groats to a small Screwfix outlet just south of Grantham where I could choose from a wide array of hardware products, all at trade prices. I realised the confusion when I spotted the name of the road, "Land's End Way." It's obvious really. How could a computer programme be smart enough to link together arguably the two most frequently paired places in Britain? Land's End and John o' Groats are essentially the geographical Morecambe and Wise of the British Isles, the cheese and pickle, Torville and Dean, the Ant and Dec – I'll be so bold as to say.

I realised my ridiculous error, specifically that of typing the name of the place to which I wanted to head, and corrected it by zooming into the map to discover that its full name was actually, "Land's End Visitor

Attraction." Once sorted, I discovered that it was a journey of around 837.27 miles, give or take .01 of a mile – a little longer when it occurred to me that we probably shouldn't cycle down the M5.

Whilst writing this book, and out of interest and a sense of nostalgia, I thought I'd see if the RAC Route Planner still existed in 2020. I couldn't really see the need for it, what with Sat Nav and smart phones but to my surprise, there it was. I typed in John o' Groats to Land's End and quickly found myself in the same industrial estate. I wondered how many foreign tourists had made the same mistake and, once back home, had entertained family members with their many photographs of timber merchants and tool hire shops, the Atlantic Ocean conspicuous by its absence.

Over the next few hours, starting from John o' Groats, I worked my way down the suggested course, tweaking it here and there, and breaking it into what I felt were sensible chunks – centred around decent-looking campsites. I also decided I wasn't going to stick to the traditional route. I thought it a wholly sensible idea to add a few miles by including a short section where we turned north again (completely the wrong way), allowing us to pass through Edinburgh. Travelling south from there, through the very heart of England rather than the usual west coast route, we could also take in Meriden (considered, at the time of our ride, to be the geographical centre of England), and visit all of our families along the way.

This would give us a break from sleeping on the ground, allow us to enjoy some homecooked meals, save a few quid and give our partners a break from the monotony of putting up and taking down a tent every day, and catering to our every whim. Of course, it hadn't yet been confirmed that they would be supporting us, but I was optimistic that they would. I mean, who wouldn't want to give up their fortnight's summer holiday to follow us around Britain on our quest for glory?

By the evening, the route was complete. In my eyes it was a masterpiece that wouldn't look out of place sitting in the Louvre, alongside the Mona Lisa and the Venus de Milo. In the end, it was 930 miles long and should take us 13 days to accomplish, although we knew, of course, that the final mileage would probably depend on diversions, on-the-spot decisions, and the occasional wrong turn. I sent it to Simon with the simple message, 'It's on.' Looking back now, I'm sure it only confirmed his initial thoughts about me.

Chapter 2: No Gear and No Idea

It was a beautiful sunny day, and we were on our bikes just outside Clevedon, a picturesque Victorian seaside town with the only Grade 1 listed pier in England. Ever wondered what that actually means? If so, you're about to find out and if not, or if you're a smart-arse and you already know, then I'd suggest skipping the next few paragraphs entirely.

As the name suggests, the building has been placed on a special list, the National Heritage List for England no less. It is in fact a rather wonderful list, as it allows us to continue to enjoy artefacts of great beauty and significance from our country's fascinating past. According to the website of Historic England, the proprietors of the list, since 1882 its task has been to protect historic buildings and sites across the country. There are now an estimated half a million such places on the list; that's a truly staggering amount and shows just how steeped in history our nation is, and how much there is to see by getting out on your bike.

Buildings and other places accepted onto the list are assigned one of three grades:

- Grade 1: Buildings of exceptional interest, of the highest significance (only 2.5 per cent of buildings on the list make this grade, so Clevedon Pier is clearly pretty special)

- Grade 2*: Particularly important buildings of more than special interest

- Grade 2: Buildings of special interest, warranting every effort to preserve them.

For those of you that love detail, the difference between 'special', 'particularly important' and 'exceptional interest' is explained in an unbelievable level of detail on the Historic England website. In simple terms, once a place is added to the list it should become very difficult to turn it into a local supermarket, or knock it down and build a multi-story carpark, or another unsightly new housing development. You know the type – where all the houses are made of cardboard, there is not a single shop, café, or anything of use to be found, and the street names are themed in an attempt to make the place sound much nicer than it is.

'Shall we take a stroll down Elderflower Drive dear and into Bluebell Way?'

'Yes dear, and let's take in Honeysuckle Road, Orchid Close and Venus Flytrap Crescent.'

Whilst unscrupulous developers seem to find a way around pretty much every obstacle, this Grade listing makes it exceptionally difficult for them to ruin our great heritage, whilst lining their pockets, and making our country that little bit uglier.

So anyway, it was now Spring, and we were on our first training ride, a fairly short run from Bristol to Clevedon and back. Simon had dusted down his old Carrera, nothing grandiose but at the very least a proper road bike, whilst I was chugging along behind on my bright yellow mountain bike. Don't get me wrong, it was a beautiful bit of kit, full suspension, fancy wheels, but if you've ever tried to ride with someone when one of you is on a road bike, and the other on an off-road machine with huge, knobbly tyres, you'll understand that they're not at all compatible. The road bike is built for speed – with its powerful gearing and slim, slick tyres – whilst the mountain bike is designed to handle, well, mountains. It's comfortable and can handle rough terrain but, on smooth tarmac, it's a fish out of water. It's like going for a Sunday drive when one of you is in a Ferrari and the other is driving a tractor.

Simon cruised along through the little villages heading towards the seaside, whilst I turned my pedals at a speed that risked starting a small fire in my trainers. He'd pull away a few hundred metres, then turn to see where I was. Observing me cycling after him, looking like a maniacal clown on one of those tiny circus tricycles, he'd shake his head and slow down almost to a stop. When I'd finally catch up, gasping for air and legs burning, he'd casually ride off into the distance and we'd repeat the process.

Just before Clevedon, we took a right-hand turn up a steep hill. 'Aha!' I thought, this is where my mountain bike comes into its own. Granted, it was no mountain, just a hill on the outskirts of Clevedon, but I thought it might level the playing field a little. How wrong I was. Simon disappeared again. I next saw him about 20-minutes later at the top. He looked like he'd been there for a while. It was time for me to get a new bike. We rolled down the hill to the seafront, had tea and cake and then rode home; Simon impatient and barely breaking a sweat, me utterly exhausted.

Before his death Mike had worked for Halfords, as had pretty much everyone in our friend group. One of them, Griff, had worked his way up to a head office role. I wasn't quite sure how, as he never seemed that organised and never returned messages. Knowing what I now know about the corporate world though, that made him perfect management material. I got in touch with him to let him know what we were doing and to see if Halfords, in memory of Mike, would be kind enough to support us in some way. In fairness to Griff, he really pulled it out of the bag (although I suspect this has a lot to do with the organisational skills of Sam, his partner at the time, who also worked for Halfords and was a great friend of Mike's). Before long we were driving up to Redditch to collect two brand new bikes which they were lending us for the duration of the ride.

I don't know if you've ever experienced love at first sight – this was the first time I can recall it. She was beautiful – lean, lithe, quick, and an incredible shade of silver. She was an Airborne: a shiny, brand-new titanium road bike, and I was smitten. We also picked up a nice new bright red Carrera. There was nothing wrong with the Carrera, and we were getting to use it for free, but it wasn't a patch on the Airborne. It was essentially a slightly newer model of Simon's current bike and, as I drove back to Bristol, I already knew we were going to have some awkward moments deciding who rode which steed.

I was itching to get out on the Airborne and give it a try. My partner at the time, Bek, was working in a marketing role for a family company based in Wells, Somerset. Wells is famous for being small. It's the fourth smallest city in the UK, in terms of population. When it comes to size, only the City of London is smaller (and that's surrounded by Greater London containing about a gazillion people). It's also famous for having a beautiful cathedral, and for being a filming location of the action-comedy movie, 'Hot Fuzz'. An eclectic mix of reasons for notoriety, sure, but it's a lovely place and well worth a visit.

A visit was what I had in mind. My plan was to cycle

there, meet Bek for lunch, and then pedal home, getting in around 50 miles in the process. I hadn't actually ridden a road bike since I was about 12 years old, when I had a very fetching bright red Raleigh bike, the type we kids referred to as a 'racer.' Since then, I had only ridden mountain bikes, and there had been a number of years where I did no cycling at all.

I set off mid-morning, full of energy, enthusiasm, and optimism. From the house it was predominantly downhill to the centre of Bristol, where I'd pick up the A37 and follow it over the Mendip Hills, all the way down to Wells. The weather was spring-like, showery one minute then very warm the next, but my spirits were high as I made decent progress through the countryside south of Bristol. When I reached the foot of the Mendips, everything changed. Mountain bikes come replete with a huge number of gears so, when the incline becomes steeper, you can simply work your way down through them until you find one that takes you slowly, but easily, to the summit.

Most road bikes, however, have fewer gears and, when you first make the transition, you'll notice how much more quickly you appear to run out of them when you head uphill. As the road began its long climb towards the treeline in the distance, I shifted down a few times, looking for a gear that would allow me a comfortable ascent. Still not quite gentle enough, I tried to move down another gear: nothing happened. I tried again, still nothing, and then I looked down and saw with horror that the reason for this was that there was nowhere left for the chain to go.

The next ten minutes or so were hard work, then I descended at speed into a valley before repeating the process. Over and over again, for what seemed like an eternity, I'd climb in the lowest gear, my legs completely sapped of energy, before very briefly getting to enjoy the recovery of the descent. I say very briefly, partly because you go so much quicker downhill, and partly because even when rolling downwards aided by gravity, I spent most of the time recoiling in horror at the next climb I could see up ahead. Then it started to rain harder.

At last, I recognised the descent into Wells and rolled in. I was sodden, exhausted, grumpy, and feeling uneasy about how hard this training ride was feeling. I met Bek for lunch – I was hoping that some food, drink, and a warm, dry place to sit would reinvigorate me, so I'd feel better for the ride home. The rain became torrential. Defeated, that afternoon I sat quietly in the corner of Bek's office whilst she worked, waiting for a lift home. I trembled with cold, or maybe it was fear as the reality of what I'd let myself in for began to dawn on me.

Of course, practice makes perfect and, with more rides and miles under my belt, I became used to the fewer gears of the road bike. It began to feel easier and I became quicker. We headed out most weekends and, over one of the Bank Holidays, achieved the training target we had set ourselves. We cycled 80 miles on two consecutive days (the average distance we would be covering each day), and then half as much again on the third day. We began to feel like cyclists, as opposed to people riding bicycles. We were ready, or so we thought.

A few weeks before we were due to set off, I'd been a little unwell. Nothing serious – just a standard case of man-flu. I'd taken it easy and decided to do a gentle gym session to ease myself back into exercise. I was doing two exercises back-to-back. One for the lower body, followed instantly by one for the upper body. For all you gym lovers, it's a method known as Peripheral Heart Action, so called because it requires you to constantly push blood to different muscles, giving your heart a good workout too. It's also a good way to build intensity whilst not overly fatiguing any one muscle group. I did a set of lunges, then grabbed hold of the bars and performed a few pull-ups.

I don't remember a great deal about what happened next, but I awoke on the gym floor to find a man, wearing the very tiniest of running shorts, stood over me asking if I was alright. Apart from my current view, I was fine, and for some reason, told him that I'd just decided to take a nap. Clearly, I was anything but fine. He pointed out that, if that had indeed been my plan, I'd chosen to fall asleep by throwing myself head-first into one of the weights machines.

People were very attentive and helpful and, after I suggested it may have been due to low blood sugar levels, the young receptionist rushed off to get me a drink, returning with a bottle of Lucozade. Unfortunately, it was one of their zero-sugar, zero-calorie range, but it was free, so I took it anyway. It wasn't often you got something for free from my gym, unless you counted the cheap headphones, rucksack and towel that were 'free' with the £30 joining fee. I'm always amazed at people's inability to spot this simple ruse, but I wonder if we've all just come to accept that most large companies will screw us over whenever and wherever they can.

I headed straight to my doctor for a check-up. He asked some standard questions and nearly blinded me when he shone his miniature torch into my eyes (which actually made me feel worse than when I'd fainted). He checked my blood pressure and took a resting ECG (an electrocardiogram, to examine my heart function). I understood a fair bit about ECGs, having had to perform them on clients in my previous health-screening job for Nuffield hospitals, so when the doctor raised some concerns I asked if I could have a peek too. 'What would you do if you saw an ECG like that?' he said.

'I'd probably send me to hospital.' I replied.

The ride was only a matter of weeks away. I was under strict instructions not to exercise and I'd been told that there would be a wait of around 12-13 weeks for the echocardiogram, the more detailed test I now needed. Over a year's worth of planning, training, and fundraising was now in jeopardy and, whilst I wanted to be safe, I wanted to do everything I could to at least make it to the start.

Fortunately, having previously worked in a private hospital came in handy and, instead of waiting 13 weeks for the test, I was able to book and pay for one to be carried out the following Tuesday. I realise private healthcare is, in many ways, elitist and only a few in society can afford the luxury. I am also in no way undermining our wonderful NHS – a benefit we are so lucky to have in this country – but I just feel that health should always be high on your list of priorities, and so if you can afford to pay to get the care you need more quickly, then do it. Hopefully, by doing so, you also help to lessen the load on the NHS, allowing those not so lucky to get their treatment more quickly. But that's just my view. You are welcome to have your own.

Five days later I was sat in the confusingly named Nuffield Chesterfield Hospital in Bristol, awaiting my test. I wondered whether there was a Nuffield Bristol Hospital in Chesterfield too. Formerly the private residence of Clifton Court, it's a beautiful manor house. I'd been lucky enough to work on the top floor, which I had all to myself apart from visiting clients, the doctor I worked with (when she was in), and allegedly the ghost of a young woman. She was the daughter of the lord of the manor and rumour has it that, after her fiancé was killed in action during the First World War, she threw herself to her death from a window on the top floor. As a child I believed strongly in all things paranormal, but with age and time spent learning about scientific matters, it would now take a lot to convince me of the existence of ghosts.

I came fairly close one dark winter's evening though, when sat at my computer in reception after finishing the day's health screens. The corridor was L-shaped, and with the reception situated on the corner, I could see both parts of the hallway. In one direction were my health screening rooms and, in the other, a series of disused rooms from a former ward, finishing at a set of heavy fire doors. I was surprised when these doors flew open and caught onto the magnetic latches that hold them to the wall, despite it being very clear there was nobody there. I was more than surprised when I went to investigate and, halfway along, found the door to one of the unused ward rooms ajar and the window wide open, even though the rooms were never used. I always suspected mischievous colleagues, but I packed up and left very quickly that evening, just in case!

The echocardiogram went exactly as I'd hoped. I received my results back from the consultant instantly, and happily they showed nothing of concern. I was fit to ride. We really were going to do this.

Whilst that obviously came as a huge relief, the result meant a lot more to me than simply the cycling challenge. I'd asked the doctor what he thought might be wrong when he'd first taken the ECG, and he'd said it was a possibility that I had HOCM – Hypertrophic Obstructive Cardiomyopathy. HOCM is a condition where the walls of the left ventricle, the main pumping chamber of your heart, become thickened. This makes it harder for your heart to pump blood and can lead to dizziness, fainting, breathlessness, and palpitations. It's a pretty serious condition and, whilst it can be managed, the doctor had pointed out that if diagnosed, I'd be unable to do any strenuous or competitive exercise.

'If that is the case, what would it be possible for me to do then Doctor?'

'Do you enjoy lawn green bowls, Mr Waters?'

All of a sudden, my head swam with thoughts of the worst-case scenario. Fitness was my passion, my identity, and my career. I'd recently started a new job teaching people to become personal trainers, a job I'd wanted to do for years, and now I was being told that I might not even be allowed to do that. I was assigned to desk duties whilst I awaited my tests and, even though it was only for a short period of time, it gave me very itchy feet. What if I really couldn't do hard exercise for the rest of my life? I wasn't sure how I'd cope with that.

It was my way of relieving stress, my way of socialising, my way of motivating and challenging myself, it was just my way. I didn't know what I'd do for a living if it turned out there had been a problem, but I did know one thing. If it turned out I had HOCM, I was going to get very good indeed at lawn green bowls.

Luckily, things turned out well. It was just a minor heart rhythm issue, and I was given the all-clear for the ride. Our thoughts returned to final preparations. It may surprise you to know that the hardest part of our planning and preparation wasn't actually the training. What challenged us the most was working out how to get four people, two bicycles, a tent, our food and a whole heap of other kit from Bristol to John o' Groats in the first place.

That's right, I said four people. The girls had admitted defeat and were 'willingly' joining us as support crew for the trip.

'So, you want us to give up all of our holiday entitlement for the rest of the year to drive the length of Britain, cooking your food, pitching a tent for you every day, and basically being at your beck and call the entire time?'

'Err, yes.'

'And what do we get in return?'

'You get to see Britain. And more importantly to be key members of our team, vital cogs in the wheel in our quest for glory.'

'Anything else?'

In the end, we had to make a lot of promises about where we'd go on future holidays, but the help we would need had been secured. The problem was that we only had a Peugeot 206 (that had first broken down 24 hours after we'd bought it) and a two-seater MR2, with a boot the size of a postage stamp, at our disposal. We could hire a car of course, but once we arrived in John o' Groats, two of us would be riding bikes all the way back, meaning a lonely and very expensive trip if the girls had to drive a vehicle each.

After countless drafts, we finally came up with this plan:

1. The girls would drive the oh so reliable Peugeot from Bristol to Edinburgh, with the bikes, tent, food, and other equipment.
2. They would then stay the night in a B&B, whilst we would fly up the next day to meet them. (I can't remember how we wangled the 55-minute flight instead of the seven-hour drive, but I think it was because Simon had genuinely convinced himself that he was part of a professional Tour de France team, and therefore that he should be treated as such. No yellow jersey wearer would expect to be cooped up, legs cramped, for the long drive to Scotland before such an important event. Whilst Kirsty would have, quite rightly,

reprimanded him for acting like a diva, she would have eventually given in just to get some peace and quiet.)

3. Once we landed, we would pick up a second hire car, and the girls would each drive one of the cars up to John o' Groats, with us as passengers. (We would be resting and mentally preparing ourselves for what lay ahead.)

4. We would camp overnight, then the next morning we'd set off heroically on the ride south. Meanwhile the girls would drive the cars back down to Inverness, dropping the hire car off at the airport, before heading north again to meet us at Dornoch Sands, the destination for the end of the first day. They would pitch the tent, prepare dinner in time for our arrival, and have a massage couch set up ready to provide foot and neck rubs to soothe our aching muscles.

From then on, the girls would share the driving of our car, supporting us if and when required, setting up camp, and being there to greet us at the end of each day as the all-conquering heroes we were.

Assuming we weren't murdered by our partners for being selfish '*%&£@~#£', which from the outset was a strong possibility, I'm sure you'll agree it was a faultless plan. What could possibly go wrong?

Chapter 3: Thank you, Alex Ferguson

'We've broken down on the M5 near Manchester.' That was what Bek rang to say, albeit with a lot more swearing. It was Friday 24th August 2007, and just a few hours since she and Kirsty had set out to drive north to Edinburgh.

It was a warm, sunny day, and we hadn't had too many of them that summer. It had hardly stopped raining, to tell the truth. Around midday we had waved the girls off, thanking them profusely for their support and generosity for about the millionth time. We were keen to make sure they understood how grateful we were to them, and even more keen to avoid them giving up halfway through and leaving us stranded in the middle of nowhere with a couple of bikes and a lot of heavy kit. After they'd gone, like the true professionals we were, Simon and I headed out to enjoy the rare afternoon sunshine in the pub beer garden, just a few doors along from Bar Amoeba, where our idea had first formed just over a year ago.

Over the years, one thing I've learned about Simon is that the more excited he gets about the imminent commencement of one of our epic adventures, the more alcohol he wants to consume. You'd think this would be detrimental, but he appears to have internal workings similar to one of those ethanol-powered, environmentally friendly buses. I don't remember what I was drinking, probably a J20 or something equally timid, but I do clearly remember seeing Bek's name pop up on my screen, as she rang to deliver the bad news about the car.

'Where are you?'

'Just south of Manchester on the M6. A long way from Edinburgh.'

'Have you called the RAC?'

'Yep. They're on their way so hopefully they can fix the problem, whatever it is.'

I reassured her that it would be absolutely fine and asked her to keep me updated. Simon and I were powerless to do anything except sit in the sunshine and chat about what (hopefully) lay ahead. Of course, nothing lay ahead if we couldn't get the car fixed, as it contained our bikes, tent, all of our other equipment and the support team. I don't remember us being particularly stressed about it, which seems insane to me now.

We remained jolly, even as Bek updated us to say that the car wasn't repairable on the roadside. Instead, they were going to have to be towed the remaining 220 miles to Edinburgh. She obviously did not sound very happy about this turn of events. We on the other hand, chose not to stress about the fact that our ride may once again be over before a single pedal had turned. It's amazing what a little sunshine, and in Simon's case, three or four pints of lager, can do for you. At around one in the morning, 13 hours after setting out, I received a text from Bek to say the car had been dropped at a garage, and that the girls had arrived at their B&B. They were not enjoying the adventure so far.

Early the next morning, Simon and I headed for the airport and the short flight to Edinburgh. The girls had already collected the hire car and, after meeting them at Arrivals, we headed straight to the garage to see what was happening with Freddie, our not so reliable Peugeot 206. In truth, French cars and I have never really got along. My very first car was a red, J-reg Renault Clio and it was lovely, until I wrote it off pulling out from a junction, having not seen an oncoming car. My second Renault Clio was not so lovely and, shortly after I'd bought it, the head gasket went, and with it the £2000 it had cost to buy. Freddie though, was the clear winner (or loser depending on how you look at it), breaking down within 24 hours of my buying him from a second-hand car dealer, at a run-down establishment just outside of Bristol.

The dealer was a strange mishmash of a typical second-hand car salesman and a pirate. Captain Arrrrrrrrthur Daly if you will. He had a broad Bristolian twang, which is surely one of the most distinctive brogues in Britain. The accent's association with pirates and piracy stems from Robert Newton's portrayal of Long John Silver, in the 1934 movie version of 'Treasure Island'. A west country man himself, Newton also used the accent when he played Blackbeard in a 1952 film, and again when reprising the role of Long John Silver for television, a few years later.

In spite of the association being a legacy of the movies, piracy does in fact have strong links to Bristol, for hundreds of years the second largest port in England, after London. Edward Teach, better known as Blackbeard, is believed to have been born in, and resided in the city. Other well-known buccaneers have connections to the area too.

The famous pirate novels, 'Robinson Crusoe,' and 'Treasure Island,' also have interesting links. Robert Louis Stevenson may have based the Spyglass Tavern, in 'Treasure Island,' on the riverside Bristol pub,' The Hole in the Wall,' whilst the Benbow Inn may have been modelled on the famous Llandoger Trow. The latter is also purported to be where Daniel Defoe, writer of 'Robinson Crusoe,' met the pirate, Alexander Selkirk, on whom the tale is based. Both pubs are still there today. The Grade II listed Llandoger Trow is a stunning building, with its black and white, wattle and daub façade, and its dark, wood-panelled interior, and thick beams. It is a shame that it's now in the hands of a well-known pub chain – akin, in my head at least, to turning

St Paul's Cathedral into a McDonalds Drive-Thru.

I rang Captain Daly to inform him that the car I had purchased from him only yesterday had broken down (the entire exhaust had fallen off mid-drive).

'Arrrrrr, shiver me timbers. I'd never try to hornswaggle ye, me hearty. Sure, he ain't ready for Davy Jones' Locker just yet! We'll heave 'im into the garage and get all-hands-on-deck to get him repaired for ye.'

After a lengthy parley, he conceded that no pieces of eight would need to change hands for the repairs. Whilst I now know that I should have just asked for a refund, I liked the colour, plus we'd already named him Freddie, and hoisted the Jolly Roger on the aerial.

Arriving at the garage, Simon and I were dismayed to see the name on the sign above the door: Alex Ferguson Motors. That name strikes fear and loathing into the heart of any Liverpool fan. Under Ferguson, Manchester United went from just seven title wins in their history to 20, two more than Liverpool's (until then) record haul. It was ridiculous. Over a 20-year period they won the Premier League a gut-wrenching 13 times, not to mention all the other trophies they amassed along the way. And it was all due to him. He bought the right players, turned completely average footballers into indispensable team members, and instilled a belief in all of his teams, over the years, that they would just keep winning. He was still firmly in place and winning things when we took on this challenge, so to see that name above the door sent shivers down our spines.

As it turned out, I couldn't have been more wrong. Alex Ferguson actually turned out to be the saviour of our entire adventure. We enquired at reception about Freddie's condition, in much the same way you might do for a relative who has been taken into hospital for a precautionary scan. We were nervous as we were well aware that the prognosis could derail our challenge completely. Mr Ferguson himself was the bearer of the bad news. Freddie, it seemed, was in a bad way. He could be repaired, but only with a number of new parts which needed to be ordered, received, and then fitted. The earliest he could be ready was Wednesday – five days from now. Our schedule was already tight; we had to stick to it in order to be back at work the Monday after we were due to finish. A loss of five days would be fatal.

We explained the situation and Mr Ferguson, rather than giving us the hairdryer treatment (a term coined by Manchester United players to refer to dressing room incidents when Sir Alex would become enraged and shout at individuals from very close range), astonished us by offering the use of one of the garage's own cars, completely free of charge. He said we could have it as a courtesy car to continue on with the challenge, and by the time we were due to cycle back into Edinburgh (by sheer coincidence and great fortune on the following Wednesday), Freddie would be ready for us to collect, and continue on our journey southwards in. It was a brand-new Peugeot 207, much nicer than Freddie if I'm honest, and it restored some of my faith in the French motoring industry, and those who work in the trade. We quickly unloaded one car, packed everything into the other and set out northwards. If ever anyone deserved the title of 'Sir Alex,' it was the owner of that car repair shop in suburban Edinburgh, not some miserable guy who happened to have won more trophies than any other football manager in history.

We were on the move, but a number of hours behind schedule, and for those of you who know Scotland, it's pretty big. North of Edinburgh, there is a whole lot more 'north.' In fact, it takes almost as long to drive to John o' Groats from Edinburgh, as it does to drive from Bristol to Edinburgh. Heading up the A9, the towns begin to thin out, and then you're hit by the breath-taking scenery of the Highlands, and the mountains of the Cairngorms National Park. Further still, you skirt Inverness, pass over the Moray Firth on the impressive Kessock Bridge, and then you're well and truly into the wilderness. A few bridges and firths later, you enter the 'really north' north (not its official title you understand), the landscape becoming ever more lunar as you do. As with all journeys to remote places, the nearer you get, the smaller the roads become and the slower you travel.

Our legs ached from sitting and it began to grow dark.

There were few other cars on the road and even fewer signs of life, barring the odd light from a distant farmhouse, and the faint silhouettes of cattle in the fields. We finally reached John o' Groats just before the last light of the day faded completely. It was chilly, decidedly windy, and even more decidedly bleak. A few buildings dotted here and there, and a flat, open plain of grass that led right up to the sea. The lack of cover meant that as soon as you stepped outside, the wind hit you hard.

'There's not much here is there?'

'Well, it is the end of Britain.'

'Why do people come here then?'

'Because it's the end of Britain. And I guess they don't stay that long.'

We checked in to the campsite and then attempted to erect the tent. We had only done one practice run, in a sunny, warm garden in Bristol. It had taken us much longer than expected. The tent was big. It had to be to accommodate the four of us, and our belongings. Trying to put up a large tent in a gale-force wind in the pitch-black when you're very tired and extremely hungry is probably about twenty times harder than you'd imagine, and I know you're imagining it sounds pretty challenging. The tent acted like a very large kite, having the tendency to lift itself high into the air, and then rather worryingly, to hurl itself towards the rocky beach and the waves beyond. We were repeatedly dragged along the grassy plain for some distance, as we desperately tried to peg the tent down. In the same way, one imagines, that Sir Ranulph Fiennes might try to secure his bivouac on an icy ledge halfway up Everest, to halt its plummet into the abyss. Well, maybe not quite the same, but it was hard work, nonetheless.

What seemed like hours later, the tent was finally up. The wind was battering the fabric, so that it appeared as if a thousand poltergeists were hammering on it simultaneously from outside. We were starving, but nobody could face attempting to light the camping stove (which we'd also never used), and it was too windy at any rate. Dinner was served shortly before midnight. Grated cheese sandwiches with ketchup. Not exactly the diet of champions, but we were pleased, and relieved, to be here, and tomorrow we would begin our attempt to cycle the length of Great Britain.

Chapter 4: A Slow Start

Day 1: Sunday 26th August.
John o' Groats to Dornoch (81 miles)

Those of you who have ever done a big event will know that often you don't sleep much the night before. It's due to a mixture of excitement, nervous energy, and sheer panic. That night, in particular, it was panic keeping me awake. It had taken us nearly eight hours, and felt exhausting, just to drive here from Edinburgh. How on Earth were we going to cycle it? What if we hadn't done enough training? What if there was another problem with one of the vehicles or, worse still, the bikes – or even worse still, with us? As these thoughts swirled around my mind, the wind ceaselessly battered the tent. It didn't make me feel any better.

One of the benefits of this nervous energy is that even though you've had little sleep, you don't wake up feeling tired; you feel pumped and ready to go from the second you open your eyes. Care must be taken to relax though, as too much adrenaline surging around your body can drain you of energy when you need it most, later on, so we decided to do a little sightseeing whilst we were there to take our minds off the challenge that lay ahead. It seemed daft to come all this way and not at least have a look around. The wind had subsided a little in the morning, and we had a proper breakfast of sausages and bacon before packing away the tent. We chose to take a quick trip to Dunnet Head, the true northern tip of mainland Britain (by car I might add, we had no desire to add miles to our challenge before it began).

I particularly wanted to see Dunnet Head lighthouse, built by the grandfather of Robert Louis Stevenson, he of 'Treasure Island' fame. Bristol, our home, was now far away, but the connection to this famous tale of pirates and adventure made it feel a little closer. Especially as we were just about to set off on our own adventure.

Headlands are strange places; bleak, exposed, weather-beaten, but at the same time, oddly beautiful, captivating, and enticing. They call you to journey to their very edges, where the land falls away sharply into the sea in a jumble of dark, jagged rocks. I guess it's the same curiosity that leads people to take on challenges like Land's End to John o' Groats. That human urge to go as far as it is possible to go. The same pull that led George Mallory (and not Edmund Hilary as many believe) to respond to the question about why he wanted to climb Everest with the answer, 'Because it's there'.

The lighthouse was bright white and surrounded by a handful of lower-lying buildings. In the distance we could make out the coastline of the most southerly of the Orkney Isles but, after just a few minutes of being battered by the winds, we were ready to head back. It had taken over half an hour to get here and we were already hungry again – a consequence no doubt of eating nothing more substantial than cheddar and ketchup sandwiches, the previous night. We stopped at a lovely little café – I can't remember its name, only that the weather was pleasant enough to sit outside with the llamas, goats, and chickens.

It was late morning by the time we made it back to John o' Groats. We readied the bikes, changed into our cycling kit, and headed toward the famous signpost to take the obligatory photographs. At the time, it was run by a private company (who also owned the equivalent sign at Land's End), and we were dismayed to discover that you had to pay to have your photograph taken, but you did get the sign personalised – with your challenge and the distance you were attempting.

I'm sat looking at that photograph now, so I can tell you a number of things with certainty. It was Sunday 26th August; it was cloudy and, judging by the number of layers we were wearing, had turned pretty cold. Simon was much chubbier than he is these days, and we had 930 miles of cycling ahead of us. After we told him about our charity fund-raising, the photographer let us take our own photographs free of charge, which I thought was very kind of him. I was saddened to learn, while researching for this book, that the original sign had gone, and with it the photography business too. I guess maybe that's what happens when most people who visit are doing something for charity, and you kindly keep giving them freebies?

The start/finish line was marked in white paint, in a rather unremarkable corner of the car park. In truth, much of John o' Groats was pretty unremarkable, but I guess that was what gave it its end-of-the-world charm. That and the stark, barren, windswept, but oddly beautiful, landscape.

I wondered whether the name had some Gaelic origin but was interested to learn, on the village website, that it was actually a derivative of a Dutch settler named Jan de Groot, who built a house there in the late 15th or early 16th century. Presumably, upon venturing this far, he was unable to face heading all the way back home. Either that or maybe he was just delighted to find somewhere that wasn't full of tourists in the summer months, so he decided to stay.

He went on to set up a ferry service to the Orkney Islands, and some allege that the small amount charged for the journey is the origin of the Groat, the now-defunct Scottish coin. It's more likely however, that the Groat gained its named from the Dutch word 'Groot', meaning great, because it was large in size. Rumour has it that he also set up a signpost and drew sketches of visitors stood next to it, in exchange for a small fee. The business developed over time into a photography enterprise, until someone ran it into the ground by giving away too many freebies. If only they'd charged a few Groats.

With a first turn of the pedals, we were off.

'It's all downhill from here,' I said to Simon, before noticing it was an instant climb out of the car park. You may remember that we'd agreed to share the bikes. The plan was to swap each day, but I'd made sure I began the ride on the Airborne. Simon was the stronger cyclist, so it made sense to try and level the playing field.

Out of the village, we were quickly on the A99 and heading south. Unfortunately, the winds (as they often do) were heading the other way. Mainland Britain's prevailing winds generally come up off the Atlantic Ocean, heading from the south-west directly for the car park at John o' Groats, or at least that's how it felt as we set off.

Many cyclists consider that the winds are the major factor in deciding the direction of travel for this most famous of challenges. This is why most people choose to start in Cornwall and ride, wind at their back, all the way north/north-east.

There were a number of reasons why we'd decided against this. Firstly, we'd assumed that, whilst the winds may be against us, the weather in general was more likely to improve the further south we went, hopefully getting warmer and drier as the ride continued. The thought of riding into increasingly cold and wet weather, as we became more fatigued, was not an appealing one. This was my thinking, anyway. Simon wasn't quite so convinced.

The second reason was logistics. We only had a few days after our scheduled finish before we had to be back at work, and it was a much shorter return to Bristol from Land's End.

The final justification was around support (and partying opportunities). Many of our friends had said they wanted to be there to celebrate when we arrived. Getting to John o' Groats to see only a goat and an old, bearded Dutchman called Jan, sat on his favourite rock, wasn't massively appealing, but a weekend camping and partying in the sand dunes on Cornwall's famous beaches most certainly was. The thought of a good party was what led Simon to agree to the southerly route.

However, a few miles on – averaging an unbelievably slow speed for the amount of effort we were expending – our choice of direction already seemed like a bad idea. It got worse when I punctured. We'd only gone five miles. At this rate I'd need 186 spare inner tubes to make it to the end. Grumbling about how the puncture was somehow my fault, Simon helped me to change the tube and we were on our way again, with him grumbling further about our choice of direction (which definitely was my fault). The road hugged the east coast, making navigation simple. All we had to do was follow two simple rules:

1. Make sure we could see the sea, with its ever-present oil rigs just off the coast, and
2. whenever we had a choice, turn left.

Other than that, I don't remember many standout moments that day. It was a constant cycle (no pun intended) of pedalling into the headwind, looking left to see oil rigs, and occasionally right to see some incredibly hairy, reddish brown Highland cattle in the fields (even the farm animals in Scotland were ginger). We were heading for Dornoch, around 80 miles away. By mile 60 we were ready to finish for the day, but we had to make it to the campsite where the girls would hopefully be by now, having dropped off the hire car and returned to pitch the tent. Time seemed to move in slow-motion, and each pedal turn became a gigantic effort. My legs were tired, they hurt, and I knew Simon felt the same as he'd gone very quiet. We were both genuinely worried that we had bitten off more than we could chew. This was only day one, and we felt physically and mentally exhausted.

Much later than we'd planned and hoped for, we turned off the A9 onto smaller roads and headed for the campsite at Dornoch. The girls were there to greet us, tent up and plenty of food and drink on hand to refuel.

'You took your time,' said Kirsty, in an attempt to lighten the mood. Simon silently climbed off his bike, looking utterly bereft of energy and emotion. Declining offers of food, he stepped into the tent and climbed inside his sleeping bag.

'I take it that it wasn't a good day?' said Bek.

Was the ride over after just one day, I wondered?

Chapter 5: Hypothermia and Midges

Day 2: Monday 27th August.
Dornoch to Fort Augustus (77 miles)

I woke early and sat outside the tent, admiring the view. Dornoch Sands was breathtakingly beautiful – in front of me lay a number of small, grass-covered dunes and beyond that, a broad expanse of golden sand. The wind had calmed. It was going to be a good day. Simon rose and seemed perkier too. For now, at least, the challenge was still on.

The girls prepared another cooked breakfast to fuel us for the miles that lay ahead. We'd decided before the ride that we'd have a full English each morning, before setting off. We were both already familiar with the technique known as 'carb-loading', where you increase intake of carbohydrates in the days before an event, whilst at the same time resting up, allowing your energy stores to be maximised.

Recently, I'd also discovered a method known as 'fat-loading', which sounded much more fun. The idea was simple – increase the fat content in your diet, causing your body to use more fats as fuels, and thus sparing carbohydrates for when you most need them. In truth, the evidence for this was limited at the time, but it was justification enough for us to have a fry-up every day, and we figured we'd be burning off the calories regardless. One thing that we definitely did notice was how much longer it kept hunger at bay. During training, we often found ourselves getting peckish very quickly after a pre-ride breakfast of porridge or muesli, but this new technique seemed to stave off the stomach pangs, possibly because of the higher protein content. Whatever the reason, we enjoyed it.

We climbed aboard the bikes, stiff and achy from the previous day's exertions riding into the headwind. I was happily still aboard the Airborne, as Simon couldn't be bothered to faff about changing pedals and seat heights. My cunning plan was working. We left the girls to pack down and catch us up, rode out of the campsite and then, about ten seconds later, it began to drizzle – the type that, as Peter Kay rightly noticed, soaks you through.

Continuing down the A9, we crossed onto the Black Isle, a peninsula just north of Inverness. At that moment, the drizzle turned into a torrential downpour. We were inexperienced cyclists, and in all honesty, ill-prepared ones too. I was wearing a pair of cycling shorts, a base layer, a waterproof (the kind suited to showers but not real Scottish rain), and a pair of trainers. I was soon soaked to the bone and freezing cold. We rode over the Kessock Bridge, even more exposed to the elements as we crossed high above the broad, dark, choppy expanse of the Beauly Firth. I began to shiver uncontrollably.

I remember seeing Inverness Caledonian Thistle's football ground beneath us, as we cycled over the bridge, descended into the city, and arrived almost at once at a retail park. There was an outdoor and adventure shop, and we decided to stop. By now I was nearly incoherent, and Simon had to guide me into the shop where I intended to buy a whole new outfit, to get warm and dry. He rang the girls to let them know the situation, whilst I selected what I needed and headed into the changing room to try it all on.

After some time had passed, Simon came to check on me. He found me sat on the changing room floor, dressed in my new gear, mumbling to myself and shaking like a leaf. He helped me up and chaperoned me to the till. Normal body temperature is 37 degrees Celsius, and it only takes a drop of a couple of degrees before symptoms of hypothermia begin to manifest. These include shivering, slurred speech and confusion. Getting indoors and changing into warm dry clothes is recommended, as is a warm drink and food, so it was excellent news when the girls arrived just after I had paid, and we decided to break for lunch. There was a pub just opposite and I can still remember the delicious salty, fatty taste of that burger and chips, washed down with plenty of steaming hot tea, while I sat wearing my new outfit (with price tags still attached).

Defrosted, re-energised, and back to my normal self, we stepped outside to continue and discovered, much to our delight, that it had turned into a gorgeous afternoon. We headed out of town, following the Caledonian Canal. It was built in the early 19th century by the famous Scottish engineer, Thomas Telford, to make it possible to travel by boat, from east coast to west coast Scotland, without having to sail around the hazardous Cape Wrath – at its northern tip.

It is actually only part canal for its 60-mile length, also incorporating four lochs along the way. We reached the first, and by far the most famous – Loch Ness – and rode along the shoreline of its foreboding dark waters. It is an impressive sight and it's easy to see how the legend of its monster has persisted since St Columba wrote of it in 565 AD, and possibly for even longer.

Stone carvings, found near the loch, etched by members of the Picts, an ancient people of Scotland, show serpent-like creatures that are strikingly similar to how we perceive 'Nessie' today. As we rode along, I imagined the legend had much to do with the surroundings. The incredibly steep-sided, dark mountains either side of the Loch plunge under the water, making it very deep indeed – Loch Ness has the largest volume of any inland body of water in the British Isles. The place has a real air of Celtic mystery. It felt like somewhere that otherworldly and prehistoric creatures would reside, probably because I'd read 'The Lord of the Rings,' one too many times. That said, so much water certainly provides plenty of space for such a large beast to hide, so you never know.

It was a very different type of monster we encountered late that afternoon. Monsters, I should say – millions of them. The infamous Highland midges were out in force. The 'Visit Inverness and Loch Ness' website informs you that they move in swarms, prefer water or marshy conditions, are mostly out early or late in the day, and prefer still, humid conditions. It was late afternoon, humid and we were riding along the banks of Loch Ness. But, the site claimed, there weren't many to be found along the banks of Loch Ness and, even if they were present, they wouldn't keep up with us whilst we were cycling, so we'd be fine.

Simon would disagree. Arriving at our campsite, in Fort Augustus at the far end of the Loch, he dismounted to discover that his arms and legs resembled a map of the solar system, with a red, itchy bite for each star. Brian Cox would have had a field day pointing out the various constellations. Upon removing his helmet, he found that he also had lines of bites running across his head, where the Midges had flown in through the vents to attack. For some reason, I remained pretty much unscathed. Maybe Scottish midges are, like some of their taller human counterparts, rather partial to the taste of alcohol.

We spent a beautiful evening on the shores of the Loch, the sun slowly dipping below the mountains to the west. We sat around and chatted whilst casually munching on sausage rolls, biscuits, crisps, and other such health-foods. This was another of our highly scientific sports nutrition techniques, known simply as 'face loading'. It involves stuffing as much food into your mouth as possible, in a desperate attempt to take on calories and feel more energetic the following day. It's both fun and surprisingly effective. Apart from that, most of the evening was spent watching Simon scratch his bites like some sort of rabid chimp, which I'll be honest, detracted from the beautiful scenery somewhat.

Chapter 6: The Last Shop for 30 miles

Day 3: Tuesday 28th August.
Fort Augustus to Pitlochry (89 miles)

Our third day began pleasantly with sunshine and stunning scenery, riding along the banks of Loch Oich, and then Loch Lochy. I appreciate that naming things can be challenging, but to name a Loch, 'Lochy' is surely the laziest of choices. It's right up there with Neville Neville, father of former Manchester United full-backs Gary and Phil.

It's hard to comprehend how it came to be that the loch was so unimaginatively named but, as we rode along its banks, I realised that it was indeed, beautifully 'lochy', an idyllic Scottish scene, and so happily forgave the naming committee for their lack of imagination. Small waves lapped against the stony shoreline, whipped up by that same old headwind, although it was not yet as strong as we'd experienced to date. On the far edge of the Loch were lush, green fields, dotted with familiar auburn-haired cattle, and beyond another range of rocky mountains rose high into the sky.

Our early rhythm was interrupted by a police roadblock. There had been a crash up ahead. It was not hard to imagine why. The sinuous roads were still wet and slippery from yesterday's rains, and there were constant fluctuations in the light, as we dipped in and out of patches of thick forest. Nothing was allowed through. Whilst this was entirely understandable, and there were far worse places in the world to be stuck, after 45 minutes we realised that we were slipping behind our schedule for the day, again. Day One had been slow due to a late start and strong headwinds, whilst Day Two had been delayed by me getting mild hypothermia – we were beginning to make a habit of it.

Eventually we were allowed to carry on our way. About half a mile down the road, I punctured for the second time on the journey. Simon couldn't hold back. He was convinced it was because I was riding too far over in the gutter.

'What are you doing, you idiot? Ride on the road rather than in the piles of rubble and debris at the side.'

He was most likely right, but I wasn't as comfortable on a bike then as I am now, and the queue of traffic that had built up behind us at the roadblock meant we were experiencing repeated close passes.

'I'd rather have a punctured inner tube than a

punctured lung.'

In my defence, my 'genius' plan worked. By the time we'd fixed the puncture, all of the cars had passed, and we once again had the road to ourselves and were able to enjoy the beautiful views.

Just after leaving the Loch we reached the impressive Commando Memorial near Spean Bridge. Yet another listed monument, it overlooks the grounds of Achnacarry Castle where the original Commando unit, formed in World War II, had trained. It is an impressive statue surrounded by equally impressive scenery, offering views of Ben Nevis and the rest of the Nevis range. We stopped for a snack and then continued on our way.

After a short while we took a turn and headed north-east – back towards John o' Groats. It may seem illogical that we were heading back in the direction we'd come, but this was the turn that allowed us to cut across to Edinburgh and collect Freddie, our temperamental Peugeot 206. We then planned to continue onwards through the centre of England, rather than using the more popular route to the west.

These were unwelcome extra miles, but the lack of road choices, principally due to the sheer volume of large, rugged mountains that stood in the way, meant that a slight detour was the only option. Scotland has two categories of mountain. The taller ones are known as Munros, after Sir Hugh Munro, who compiled the original list in the late 19th century. Rather amusingly I think, the smaller hills have recently been termed, Marilyns.

We were on an A-road, but you'd never have known. It was narrow, rural and we saw not a single car. We rode past a local store with a sign outside that said: 'Last shop for 30 miles.' We laughed at the ridiculous tactics some retailers go to in order to get people to spend money in their establishment. Soon though, we realised that they weren't exaggerating, as we rode along arguably the most stunning stretch of road we'd ever cycled.

There really were no shops. No cars. No people. In fact, there was nothing. Well, nothing but forest-covered mountains that rose high to our left, and the pure blue waters of Loch Laggan shimmering away in the sunshine to our right. There was total silence save for a few birds and the sounds of our bikes. It was as close to heaven as you could imagine. I think we sometimes forget how very beautiful our little island is, especially the mountainous regions of Wales and Scotland.

Nothing is on quite the scale to be found in other parts of the world. The mountains aren't as high, the lakes not as big, the forests not as vast or soaring as high overhead as those in North America say, but none of this detracts from their beauty. Seeing it on a bike makes it even more special. It gives you the time to take it in and the chance to not only see, but to hear and smell it too – to be miles from anywhere, totally immersed in nature. This was exactly what I wanted from our adventure.

Very occasionally we passed large, impressive houses – real rural hideaways. A helicopter was landing in the grounds of one, and we joked that it was probably how people received home shopping in these parts. We'd already passed a number of Lidl supermarkets in the first few hundred miles and, mostly due to the hysteria that sets in when you spend so much time with someone doing the same thing hour after hour, we'd soon created a song about this. Here's how it went (to the tune of 'Little by Little,' by our favourite band, Oasis):

Lidl by Lidl, they drop your shopping off by helicopter, Lidl by Lidl, the wheels on our bikes are slowly going round.

I say song but we only got as far as a second line. This became a big problem, not because we expected to release it and have a hit, but because it was stuck in our heads for the entire rest of the journey, all 700 miles of it. It was sung out loud every time we passed a discount supermarket, and sometimes one of us would burst into song for no other reason than it passed the time. It became our ride equivalent of, 'The Wheels on the Bus' (which is inevitably going to be going round and round in your head all day now, for which I'm very sorry).

We finally turned south again, and the road became hillier, weaving left, right, up, and down, again and again. It was like a rollercoaster but without the fun, screams and, thankfully, the vomiting. Tiring, as the end of another day approached, we reached the busy A9, passing places with incredibly Scottish names like Dalwhinnie, Aldclune and – my favourite – Killiecrankie – which brought to mind bizarre visions of an ancient bloody battle between the clans, only with one army dressed in school uniforms, like one half of that most cringeworthy 80s comedy duo.

It was getting busy. Lorries roared by, loudly blasting their horns at us as if we had committed some terrible crime by daring to share their road. It was, frankly, terrifying – worse than anything the Krankies had ever done. There was a cycle path to the side, but it was badly overgrown with thorny bushes and, in places, the tarmac had crumbled away. It looked more like the remnants of a lost civilisation than a usable cycle route.

We were left with no choice but to get our heads down and go for it. Thankfully, it was largely downhill, and we were soon on calmer local roads, following the signs for Pitlochry. Our phones had run out of battery, and we hadn't had the foresight to bring paper maps, so we stopped to ask directions from the first person we saw. Imagine, if you will, a caricature of the most Scottish-looking young man you can. Now swap out the kilt and bagpipes for a more normal outfit, and you're pretty much there. His hair was the brightest orange you could conceive, and his skin was so pale as to be almost translucent. I asked him for directions to the campsite, and he looked at me as if I was enquiring about which way it was to the moon.

'Awa' an' bile yer heid. Ye cannae cycle there,' he said, and then strangely, in perfect English, 'It's way too far!' I learned much later exactly what he was saying – basically that this was a daft proposition and clearly impossible. At the time, whilst unsure of the precise meaning, I did at least understand that he felt the task might be beyond us. I insisted that we could probably make it (given that we'd ridden nearly 250 miles in the last three days to reach this point) if he could just be so kind as to point us in the right direction. Three or four miles later, we made it to the campsite. In all fairness to our navigational assistant, there was a short, reasonably challenging hill on the way that, to the uninitiated cyclist, might well have felt like cycling up the north face of the Eiger.

The campsite was beautiful, nestled between the lush green forests and hills of the Loch Tummel National Scenic Area. We spent another pleasant evening relaxing our tired limbs, whilst continually grazing from the buffet selection provided by our wonderful support crew. We were still on track and beginning to believe in our ability to pull this off.

Chapter 7: A Comfy Bed in Edinburgh

Day 4: Wednesday 29th August.
Pitlochry to Edinburgh (77 miles)

During challenges like this, you might assume that you become more tired with each passing day, but that's not always the case. We were exhausted after the first day and incredibly achy when we set off the following morning, but Day Three felt easier, and I awoke on Day Four feeling relatively fresh. It doesn't simply become gradually harder over time. Instead, you are taken on a pain and energy rollercoaster. Sometimes you feel utterly spent and unable to turn the pedals even one more revolution, then five minutes later the sun breaks through the clouds, or an amazing vista opens up before your eyes, and you are completely recharged, as if somehow plugged into nature itself. Pain can be excruciating one minute and then, all of a sudden, vanish as if it were never there.

For no good rhyme or reason, the pain also tends to move around your body. One moment it's your knee that's hurting, then that stops, and the pain travels up into your shoulders as if it were a living entity on the move inside you. Weirdly, when it shifts somewhere else, this comes as a pleasant relief. At least it's different, you think to yourself. You smile, carry on, and then 100 metres up the road, you're grimacing again.

When things get really bad, you find yourself resorting to all sorts of pain and fatigue management methods. Saying to yourself, *I'll get to 40 miles and I'll see how I feel*, or, when it's worse, *let's just make it to that lamppost up ahead, then I'll stop*. But you don't, of course, you just target another lamppost a little further along. In really desperate times, you start to count – *I'll do 20 pedal turns*, you say to yourself but, once done, you reset to zero and start again. You know it's bad when you start aiming for less than ten, but you keep going regardless.

That morning we both felt pretty good and we set off at a reasonable hour, bound for Edinburgh, our overnight stay where we'd be picking up Freddie. We prayed that he'd encounter no further issues on the journey. The A9 was horribly busy again, so we paused to look at the maps and followed some smaller lanes that ran parallel.

It made for much more pleasant riding, apart from when we passed one small farmstead that was surrounded by metal gates, covered in barbed-wire and threatening signs with foreboding messages like 'We're watching you,' 'We know what you're up to,' and 'The dogs haven't been fed for days…they're hungry.' The canines in question were three big, aggressive black dogs that sat with their faces pressed right up against the wire fence. They barked continuously and salivated uncontrollably. They ran alongside us as we rode, I hoped that the fence wasn't going to suddenly come to an end and leave us pedalling like our lives depended on it (which they very much would have).

After we were out of range of the CCTV, and rifles in the guard towers, we relaxed and enjoyed the countryside that led us all the way into Perth – a pretty little town – where we stopped for a very pleasant lunch with the girls.

The A9 finally headed off in a different direction, and our afternoon was spent navigating smaller roads – bound for the Firth of Forth. It was either that or pedal straight along the M90, which we didn't think the Scottish traffic police would take kindly to. I remember some years later reading about four members of the Sri Lankan cycling team, in Glasgow for the Commonwealth Games, who had been caught riding along the M74. It's probably quite a nice surface to cycle on, but likely spoiled by the ever-present prospect of death.

We trundled through lush, green rolling hills and farmland, the landscape now so strikingly different from the high peaks, heather, and lochs of the Highlands. It was pretty, but not in the striking way of the wilderness, which captured our attention at every turn. Eventually, we reached the Firth of Forth and rode high above the waves on the cycle path over the Forth Road Bridge.

I don't particularly like heights, so I've never enjoyed riding across bridges like this – open and exposed to the elements. It was very breezy up there, but for once I felt fortunate that we had a headwind, so I only had to be concerned with pedalling harder, and not worry about being blown towards the edge of the bridge from where I could see the freezing cold water, hundreds of feet below. I was perfectly safe of course. The railings were plenty high enough but, when you have a fear of heights, that doesn't stop your mind from imagining some freak gust of wind picking you up and carrying you to your doom.

We reached the other side and headed east into Edinburgh to meet up with the girls at our B&B for the night. This was situated directly underneath Arthur's Seat, the long extinct volcano that sits at the heart of Holyrood Park, a stone's throw from the parliament building, castle and city centre. The girls had collected Freddie from Sir Alex (fully repaired, and for a very generous price too) and had once more painstakingly transferred all of our belongings from the courtesy car.

We were extremely grateful for their help, and possibly just as grateful that our afternoon spent navigating the smaller roads had slowed us down sufficiently not to have to do any of the work ourselves.

One of the interesting psychological aspects of big challenges like this is that you assign all of your energy to the physical elements of the event. As soon as you are done for the day, it's like your body goes into standby – even simple tasks like opening a can of food, or having to fetch a pair of socks from the boot of the car, begin to feel gargantuan. You simply whine pathetically about how tired you are in the hope that someone will do it for you. It is not an endearing trait, but I guess your brain is in survival mode, only wanting to use energy when it absolutely has to.

That evening we headed for a nearby Italian restaurant and enjoyed a tasty pizza washed down with a glass of red wine. We had decided to celebrate our achievements so far by treating ourselves to our first alcoholic beverage of the trip. Afterwards, we retreated to our B&B and slept soundly in comfortable beds for the first time on the journey.

I love Edinburgh. It's a wonderful, vibrant city (if a little chilly most of the time). I would have loved to have spent a day walking its streets, full of grand, ornate, buildings – unusually dark due to the local granite used to build them. And then to wander up the steep cobbles of the Royal Mile, a mediaeval street taken straight out of a fairy-tale, to the castle gates. That would have to wait for another time. We had another long journey ahead of us tomorrow. It was time to head back to England.

Chapter 8: The First and Last

Day 5: Thursday 30th August.
Edinburgh to Border Forest (65 miles)

It's funny how people imagine Scotland to be such a small part of the UK. Here we were, starting day five of thirteen, and we were still in it. A number of the companies I've worked for over the years have divided Great Britain into regions for operational purposes – the South East (often with London as a separate region), the South West, the Midlands etc. In all of those companies, Scotland was treated as a single region, even though its land mass accounts for over thirty per cent of the United Kingdom, and it is well over half the size of England. Its population is only a tenth of England's, but imagine if we simply lumped over half of England under the banner of one regional identity. Simon actually does this, by considering everyone from above the M4 to be a northerner, but we shouldn't all think like him. I wonder if this marginalised view of Scotland has its roots in the London-centric outlook held by our government, the media, and other institutions? Whatever the reason, I think it's a shame, and it certainly doesn't make it any smaller to cycle through.

I was sad to be leaving behind the amazing views, but excited to feel that we were really making progress. We left Edinburgh on the A68, heading south for the stunning town of Jedburgh, home to a grand abbey, castle, jail, and the Mary Queen of Scots Museum. One of the regrets I was having about our adventure, or rather, something I thought I'd do differently on the next one, would be to take our time more, to stop and explore places. Our entire ride was focused on getting from one place to the next as soon as possible, always with somewhere to be by a certain time, and never a chance to just stop and look around. I'm sure I could easily spend half a day or more exploring Jedburgh but, for now, all I could do was steal fleeting glances as we rolled on by. Looking back on this, I feel it's a product of youth – back then the challenge lay in achieving the distance at a reasonable speed. I guess you mellow somewhat as you get older, you also lose a bit of pace, and both factors serve to make you look at trips such as this in a different way.

The hills were smaller now than they'd been further north, but the undulating terrain was aggravating my knee. It had been hurting since Loch Ness. The pain was gradually intensifying, and lasting longer each day. I was still on the Airborne, because as I'd mentioned previously, Simon couldn't be bothered to faff around changing over the pedals and adjusting the set-up. This made me very happy, but I was convinced the toe-clips I was using were the cause of my problems. Simon, being the more experienced cyclist, was wearing proper clip-in pedals, but I'd not been brave enough to try them in training, and didn't want to start doing something new during the ride.

As the road headed once more skywards, my knees began to hurt a lot. I decided to stop and do something about it. When we reached a flatter section, I went to pull over. I failed to get my feet out of the straps, as I had them done up so tightly, and slowly tumbled sideways onto the grassy bank by the side of the road. It was a comfortable landing. In fact, I hadn't fallen far at all. The bank was quite high and so I was lying at a 45-degree angle, feet still strapped in firmly and unable to move. Luckily, there were no cars around, and Simon had been in front, so there were no witnesses to my comedic fall. I shouted Simon to stop, and he turned back to help free me from my predicament, chuckling to himself, and with a puzzled expression on his face.

'How did you manage that, fella?'

We removed the straps and toe-clips completely and rode onwards, my feet now just resting on the flat pedals. It was less efficient, but my knees never bothered me again on the ride.

The road continued to climb all the way to the English border, and then we were swept downwards, absolutely flying, surrounded by thick forest on all sides. It was as if Scotland had been a land in the sky, like Laputa in Gulliver's Travels, and we were descending now to the earthly realm of England far below. In fact, we were riding the road between Kielder Forest on one side and Northumberland National Park on the other. It was exquisite; another one of those moments where energy surges through your pores into your muscles, your bones, and your very soul. The thick pine forests passed in a blur of green. We sped along the banks of Catcleugh Reservoir, continuing to soar ever downwards, or at least that's how it felt.

We flew past a turning for a campsite.

'Wasn't that where we're staying tonight?'

'Nah. The girls said it was a good few miles over the border and we've only just crossed into England.'

'Ok cool. Onwards and downwards.'

When we noticed the forest thinning and the road flattening out, we pulled into a pub car park to check the map. The campsite was indeed the one we had passed - five miles back in the other direction, uphill all the way. Not fancying this much, Simon decided we should ring the girls to get them to pick us up. Surely that was one of their duties as support crew? I rang Bek, wary of the likely response.

'Hey. We've missed the turning for the campsite, and

we're five miles further down the road. It was much nearer to the border than you thought. It's a steep climb, so we wondered if you'd come to pick us up?'

'We've not been here long, and the tent isn't even up yet. Can't you ride back up?'

Simon was listening in to the conversation and decided to interject. He asked me to pass him the phone: 'Look, we've missed the turning because of your cruddy directions. Will you come and get us, please?' he said.

'We can, but we still have to prepare dinner, and we don't want to be eating late, again!'

'Whoa, you've really let yourselves down today.'

'What the…You better be careful what you're saying, or you'll definitely be cycling back up that hill.'

I quickly took the phone back before things got out of hand. 'If you can come and pick us up whenever is convenient for you, we'd hugely appreciate it.'

'Ok. See you in a bit.'

She hung up. Her tone of voice was enough to tell me that they were less than pleased. There was always much for them to do in the evenings, and they had just started to relax for the first time on the journey after spending the day enjoying a boat cruise off the coast – to see the Puffins at Farne Island. Simon was delighted that they were coming to collect us, and even more delighted that they would be a while, as it meant our only option was to head into the pub.

Inside the First & Last Inn, we were greeted by a

barman who was the spitting image of Michael, the Geordie character from the Alan Partridge series. Not only did he look just like him, but he sounded like him too. Simon ordered a pint and I asked for a blackcurrant and lemonade, and we got talking to the barman about our adventure so far. We told him we had overshot our campsite and were delighted when he suggested we lock our bikes up inside the pub that night, come back to collect them first thing, and start the next day from where we'd left off. This meant we were now ahead of schedule, so Simon celebrated with another pint whilst we waited for the girls to arrive.

On reflection, this may have been the point at which the cracks in the relationship between riders and support crew began to emerge. Tiredness can often lead to impatience and Simon's attempted reprimand hadn't gone down too well. Still, they came to pick us up and we headed back to the campsite for dinner, wishing farewell to the barman, still afraid to ask after Alan Partridge. We were after all just a stone's throw from Newcastle. Instead, we asked him what tomorrow's route was like. We would be continuing along the A68, heading for Yorkshire, and wanted to get an idea of what was in store. He responded by drawing a series of steep wavy lines with his hand; the sort of gesture you make when you're trying to describe the sea on a particularly rough day, and then proceeded to warn us about the motorbikes. *He's exaggerating*, we thought.

Chapter 9: The Road to Hell

Day 6: Friday 31st August.
Border Forest to Osmotherley (92 miles)

After a couple of hours on our bikes, we knew that the barman had not been exaggerating. If anything, he had understated the full horror of the situation. We would climb short, incredibly steep hills that required a huge amount of effort, only to plunge back down instantly, and then repeat the torture again and again. To make matters worse, we must have been passed by well over 100 motorbikes, all screaming by at ridiculously dangerous speeds. It was as if we'd somehow accidentally stumbled into the middle of the Isle of Man TT. In short, it was hell.

I feared for my life on more than one occasion, so when we reached what seemed like a reasonably large town at lunchtime, I was grateful to stop. Tow Law is a former mining town and iron works west of Durham, with a population of around 2,000. We found a pub, went inside, and stood by the bar, waiting to be served. Across the room, a man and woman were sat, drinking and smoking. The smoking ban had been enforced a few months earlier in England, news that clearly hadn't reached this far north just yet. We waited patiently to be served. A few minutes went by before the lady finished her drink, stubbed out her cigarette, and stood up to address us.

'What can I get you both?'

Taken aback by this remarkable level of customer service, I enquired if they were still serving lunch. The pair looked at each other before the lady replied (and I make no exaggeration here, these were her exact words),

'What makes you think we do that sort of thing?' Aside from stating the obvious – that from first impressions we appeared to be in a pub – a type of establishment known for its purveying of food and drinks – I wasn't sure what to say, so instead I just asked if they knew of anywhere in town where we might get something to eat. They looked at each other in a state of confusion, shrugged their shoulders, and we hurriedly left. Not only had news of the smoking ban not spread this far yet, but it also seemed that the idea of providing sustenance, that wasn't liquid and alcoholic, was still one for the future.

'Wait until they find out about mobile phones, it will kill them,' muttered Simon.

Heading further into town we came across the High

Street. On one side was an Off-Licence, in and out of which travelled a steady stream of bikers, filling the inside pockets of their leathers with bottles of beer, before climbing back aboard their bikes.

On the other side of the road was a local shop. We had no bike locks, so I popped my head through the door and enquired whether it would be alright to leave our bikes in the large empty space just inside the door (and well out of the way), whilst we shopped. This request was met with a short, sharp, 'No,' which I suppose was fair enough, or else they might have had hairy bikers requesting the same accommodation for their Harley Davidsons. Instead, we took it in turns to go in and purchase something from the selection of chocolate, sweets, and crisps which, according to the sign above the door, constituted a grocery store.

We ate our snacks and climbed back on the bikes, more fearful than ever of the motorcycle road race we were stuck in, and which now appeared to be fuelled by a well-known local dark ale. I don't think I've ever been to a more desolate town before or since. It struck me as England's equivalent of the Wild West, except that the mines had been full of coal, the gold of the North-East. These were of course long gone, as were the iron works and as is so often the case, a loss of industry meant a loss of work and hard times for the locals. On reflection, I guess it was understandable if no one had been exactly thrilled to see us pass through.

Leaving town, we were still starving and on the lookout for somewhere to eat. After only a few minutes we saw a sign for a posh-sounding hotel, a conversion of a former stately residence, called something or other Manor. It looked a little above our normal budget, but the sign clearly stated that the restaurant was open to visitors, so we rode our bikes up its grand, sweeping, tree-lined driveway.

The reception was one of those dark, oak-panelled lobbies, where even the air seems old and important. We looked rather out of place in our cycling shorts and waterproof jackets, particularly me, as I was wearing a luminous yellow number that was covered in dirt and bike oil. There were a number of people milling around, all smartly dressed, and we were disappointed to discover that the restaurant was closed for the day, as there was a wedding taking place.

By good fortune, the fathers of the bride and groom were in the lobby. One had a Geordie accent and the other spoke with a strong Irish lilt. It wasn't easy to understand either of them, but their tone, body language, and beaming smiles told us they were kindly gentleman. They came over and, upon learning about our challenge, and our desperate need for food, they very kindly assured us that they would sort something out. We were taken aback when they invited us to sit at the top table with the wedding party. Here, still dressed in our Lycra and grubby luminous attire, we enjoyed the three-course wedding breakfast and a slice of the wedding cake. Simon gave an impromptu and quite rude speech, toasting the bride and groom, and then we drank and danced the night away before retiring to a complimentary luxury twin suite – our heads a little sore but feeling much better than when we'd arrived.

None of that actually happened of course, except the offer to sort us out some food. We were shown to a small side-room where we could sit, out of the way of the wedding party. Here we were served a very pleasant lunch of sandwiches, crisps, and tea, and then we set off again, re-energised and very much obliged for the hospitality and kindness.

There was no obligation to take any notice of us on what would be, to some present, the most important day of their lives. Many would have regarded us as intruders. I wish we had the names of the people responsible, so I could thank them in print. Needless to say, our view of the people of Tow Law was very much improved by this act of generosity, and it suddenly seemed a much nicer place.

We were cheered up further by the fact that the roads became less hilly, and a lot quieter, after lunch. Once we'd made it past Darlington, it became quite a pleasant afternoon. It was never really sunny or warm, but the rain wasn't too heavy either. It was quintessential British summer weather of the type that can best be termed, 'changeable'. We were headed south-east now, our target a campsite perched on the very edge of the North York Moors, in a place called Osmotherley.

This part of Yorkshire is blessed with many place names that sound fantastic when you run them through your mind in the strong local accent – Allerton Mauleverer, Carlton Husthwaite, Wharram Percy, Kirby Grindalythe, and Wetwang. Wetwang was made famous by the late, great, host of 'Countdown,' Richard Whiteley, whose repeated humorous mentions of the village on the show led to him being made its honorary mayor, for the seven years preceding his premature death in 2005.

With our wangs and other body parts relatively dry, we neared our destination. What we hadn't counted on was that there would be a fair climb to the campsite. Knowing the North York Moors better these days, as I do, it's a good bet there'll be a tough climb if you're heading anywhere in the area. At the time though, we had been less well acquainted with them, and it wasn't what either of us needed after our longest day on the bikes so far. Heading up the climb, the girls caught us up. They were just arriving after another long day of support duties.

For any of you considering, or being cajoled into, a support role on an event like this, let me say categorically that it is not at all easy. In fact, in many respects, it is harder than doing the actual event. Days are long and involve a series of menial tasks including food prep and washing up, erecting a tent, and taking it down again. In fact, on multi-day trips, you'll put up and take down a tent so often that the most interesting part of your day becomes how quickly you can do it. There is a lot of driving, not always on the beautiful roads that your team are enjoying. On some days you may need to get ahead of them or track them down – to drop off much needed kit or emergency supplies, which can mean shuttling along busy A-roads and motorways.

You will spend hours visiting supermarket stores up and down the country, buying ridiculous amounts of food and drink because the team are getting through it like a pack of rabid gremlins. And, to top it all, your 'athletes' won't be anywhere near as grateful as they should be, because much of the time they're tired, wet, cold, hungry, or in pain (and often all of the above). Well, that was our excuse anyway. It's certainly no holiday, and demands extraordinary degrees of forbearance on your part – the phrase, 'the patience of a Saint' springs to mind. You will certainly be tested on occasion. And by occasion, I mean every single day.

Our rendezvous with the girls, just short of the campsite was, unfortunately, one such occasion. Finishing the day before in the pub had quenched Simon's thirst for a rewarding end to each day. He had therefore earlier requested a packet of cigarettes be bought and made available to him when we arrived in

Osmotherley. He was a little grumpy when he discovered that this request had been overlooked, and therefore failed to appreciate or acknowledge the wide range of support that had been provided that day, just as every day. The girls had shopped for all the food and water and were just about to begin putting up the tent for the seventh time, but a fatigued Simon let them know of his displeasure that they had not also stopped for forty Marlboro Lights. This small tantrum was met with taunting laughter by the girls and he was, politely, told that in future, if he wanted cigarettes, he should buy them himself.

As they drove away up the hill at speed, their laughter echoed around the peaceful, rolling green fields. Simon rode up the hill in a foul mood, grumbling about the incident to let off steam, whilst I trundled along behind silently, head down.

We arrived at the campsite entrance atop the hill, and our mood rose slightly when we discovered that our pitch was tucked away in the bottom corner. We got to enjoy a rather cool descent, zigzagging through sweet-smelling pine forest until we saw the familiar sight of the car, and the girls putting up the tent with the same speed and finesse of those who pull tablecloths clean from under a fully laden silver service. The incident was quickly forgotten and further conversations about cigarettes were diplomatically avoided that evening.

It wasn't long though before I was having a tantrum

of my own. For dinner, the girls had prepared fajitas. Under normal circumstances, I'd have been delighted, but I was tired and hungry. Every time I attempted to assemble a fajita, I overfilled it and the contents would spill out before I was able to get it to my mouth.

'I f*@%#ng hate fajitas!' I shouted, rather more loudly than I'd anticipated. Some evil stares from parents in neighbouring tents put me back in my place and I silently went about reassembling my dinner. Still, we enjoyed our evening in beautiful surroundings and the sun even came out to help fully dry out our wangs and other hard to reach parts.

Chapter 10: Shove Your Coat Up Your #*%@

Day 7: Saturday 1st September.
Osmotherley to Worksop (89 miles)

The great thing about an uphill finish to a day is that you get to start the next with a downhill. That would have been true today of course – if we hadn't been right at the bottom of the campsite. The climb back out was hard work, our muscles were cold and stiff, and I noticed that it was taking longer each day to get into 'the zone.' I say, 'the zone', as if suggesting that we were reaching some place where our mental and physical performance was at its peak, but what I'm actually referring to is simply the point at which things stopped hurting, or at the very least, became bearable. It was often very much about controlled misery and discomfort.

We made it out of the campsite, cruised downhill to the main road and turned left onto the A19, headed for York. To our delight, and for the only time I can recall on the entire journey, we had no headwind. In fact, unless I was very much mistaken, the wind appeared to be behind us, pushing us along. It wasn't even raining. We absolutely flew the 35 miles or so to York, working as a pair on our own mini team time-trial. For once ahead of schedule, we arrived in the former Viking and Roman stronghold of York where we were meeting the girls for lunch. Sadly, this was as good as our day was going to get.

Rolling into the centre, we reached a set of traffic lights just as they turned red. Simon was tired and (experienced cyclists, you know what's coming next) failed to unclip properly from his pedal, falling sideways almost in slow motion. He continued to block oncoming traffic as the lights changed to green. I helped him up, both of us laughing at the slapstick nature of the fall, and then we stood by the side of the road surveying the damage.

With only his pride hurt, and the score for comedy falls now at one a piece, we readied ourselves to continue, but then I noticed a bike shop across the road. I thought I would use the opportunity to upgrade my cycling shorts. I'd reached that point of the ride where my undercarriage area was never really comfortable. It simply alternated between being a little painful, extremely painful, or numb and tingly. Whilst numbness was preferential to pain, the chance to purchase something that may offer some relief, and prevent me having to constantly shift in the saddle, was one I couldn't pass up.

We enjoyed a very pleasant lunch with the girls in one of York's many lovely tea rooms. It really is a delight of a city, steeped in history and with quirky old buildings left and right – often leaning left and right too. Kirsty's brother, Patch, had turned up to show his support and that probably helped to alleviate tensions that had been brewing since the 'cigarettes incident' of the previous evening. After lunch, Patch took some team photos and the girls asked if we needed anything from the car before setting off, as they were going to head for the campsite and begin putting up the tent (yet again). We topped up our drinks and snacks but decided against taking additional clothing, as the weather remained pleasant and the skies looked clear.

We set off across a flat plain, headed for Doncaster. On both sides we could see the ghastly cooling towers of power stations, one of the ugliest reminders of mankind's impact on our planet. Tall, dark, and gloomy, to my mind they belong firmly in some sort of Orwellian dystopia, not the lush, green farmland of Britain, or anywhere else for that matter. Perhaps we could at least get Banksy, or someone, to paint some cool artwork on the sides and brighten them up a bit?

As if reading my mood, the sky became equally dark and gloomy. It looked like it might rain. Simon, deciding that he might need his coat after all, pulled into a layby, rang the girls and, in his not-so-subtle manner, requested that they drive to our location to deliver it. They agreed, but I can't say that they were entirely happy about it.

It took them an age to find us, and they kept ringing every five minutes to check where we were. We had not moved from the spot where we had called them, but for some reason, they struggled to locate us.

What followed we now refer to as 'Coatgate'. The girls arrived, pulling up abruptly next to us. They were annoyed that they had struggled to find us, but we had been where we had said all along. I think Simon had become a little cold and frustrated at having to wait for them to arrive too.

'It's ok Kirsty,' said Simon. 'Thanks for coming to find us, but I don't need my coat anymore – looks like the weather is clearing up.' This tipped Kirsty over the edge. She threw Simon his coat, in the same breath unleashing the most impressive barrage of abuse I have ever heard, not for the swear words you understand, but the varied and little-used prefixes.

'You obdurate $£@~#', and 'you vexatious *&@?', were two of the more memorable insults. It was as if the rudest thesaurus ever produced was being read aloud. She waved her arms at him throughout, expending more energy than we had probably used in cycling that day. And the funniest thing – Patch was there recording it all for posterity, with a selection of photographs that perfectly reflected the mood.

In the end, Simon was right. It didn't rain, and so the coat wasn't even required. Wisely, he decided to keep hold of it rather than ring the girls and ask them to come and take it back, as he may have had it inserted somewhere that would have made my undercarriage issues look trifling by comparison.

We arrived in Doncaster and were met with a huge number of road choices at one of the largest roundabouts I have ever seen. As we had done in Scotland, we asked a local gentleman for directions towards Worksop. We were met with the sort of incredulous look that we were becoming accustomed to. Presumably on this occasion because Worksop was twenty miles away, or maybe the gentleman simply thought Worksop unworthy of a visit, especially one that involved the effort of cycling all the way there.

It does amaze me, though, how frequently I experience this kind of response. It is as if human beings have forgotten what those two dangly things beneath them are there for. I once asked directions to a hotel, from a small train station just outside of Leeds. I knew it was no more than a mile away, and had a vague idea where it was situated but, because my phone battery had died, I lacked precise directions. The looks I received were astonishing – it was as if I was asking the way to the summit of Everest whilst dragging an old iron bathtub along behind me. In fact, all I possessed was a small suitcase with wheels, and a desire to stroll to my destination rather than pay for a taxi.

Therein lies the problem though, I suspect. Our lives are so automated, nowadays, that we don't actually need to perform a great deal of physical activity. We have cars and Uber, computers for work instead of manual labour, a range of devices that enable us to communicate with someone without physically moving, dishwashers and spin driers that do the housework for us, and ultimately even medication we can take to mitigate the illnesses we get from spending too much time sat on our behinds.

The mindset for many has become one of, *how do I do this with the least effort possible?* A thought process that, in fairness, was useful in our less evolved state, when food was scarce, and we needed to conserve energy to hunt and fend off our enemies. These days, however, it is our nemesis. I've read numerous scientific studies that show the average Briton moves for just twenty minutes a day, or often even less. That's a staggeringly small amount, almost a challenge itself to achieve. A small band of us, though, for whatever reason – maybe upbringing or genetics – still prefer physical effort and actually enjoy the breathlessness, pain and discomfort that comes with pushing our bodies to their limits. If you'd like to see a humorous take on modern man's lack of desire to move, type 'Stuck on an escalator,' into YouTube.

Our ears ringing with warnings of impending doom about the perilous journey we faced ahead, and the strong likelihood that we'd never make it, we headed off along the right road and made surprisingly good time to the campsite. The reception from the support crew was a little frosty, but luckily the site was pretty and peaceful, and the sun shone enough that evening to thaw everybody out quickly. We also agreed we'd carry our waterproofs on us at all times from now on, just in case.

Chapter 11: Cycle Lanes are for Pussies

Day 8: Sunday 2nd September.
Worksop to Redditch (100 miles)

The headwind was back. This was especially unfortunate as we were heading directly into it for over 100 miles today, our longest planned ride and the only 'century' of the entire journey. The goal was to make it to my hometown of Redditch, to enjoy a night of home-cooked food and comfortable beds, our first since Edinburgh.

We headed south towards Nottingham. Progress was slow, and we really needed to make good time. Unfortunately, the temptation of a few extra minutes in bed grows ever stronger the further you get into a trip such as this. You then proceed to get ready much more slowly, partly because you're tired and aching, and partly because you're well aware what it will be like once you climb into the saddle. We'd been guilty of this too often now. The lateness is then compounded when you encounter mechanical issues, or traffic problems, during the day. Add to that longer than necessary snack breaks and lunches, and you find yourself finishing way too late, making it likely that the cycle (pun intended) repeats itself the following day.

We rode through what is left of the once gigantic Sherwood Forest, home to the fabled Robin Hood. It's now only a thousand acres but is known to have covered an area a quarter the size of Nottinghamshire when the Domesday Book was collated. Whether Hood existed at all is a topic of much debate. Even if he did, versions of the tale have him hailing from York, Wakefield, and even further afield, so he and his Merry Men may never have resided there at all. We managed to pass through without bandits taking any of our possessions to give to the poor; we saw no maids or drunken friars and, disappointingly, the only men in tights were out for a morning jog.

A little further along, and much later than planned, we arrived in the eponymous city of Hood's famous nemesis – the Sheriff of Nottingham. We didn't see him this time, or rather her I should say – for, at the time of our trip, the Sheriff's name was Jeannie Packer. We had intended to plough straight through the centre of town, but the roads were heavily backed up and it was stop-start every few metres.

After looking at the maps, Simon suggested we head out onto the ring road and re-join our route south of the city. We did so and began to pick up speed but, once we were on a dual carriageway, I noticed a sign that said bikes should leave at the next exit and join a cycle path. Simon insisted we ignore it. A bit further along, more signs confronted cyclists with the warnings, 'Last Exit Before Impending Doom', 'Beyond Lies The Point of No Return', 'You're Going to Die, you Illiterate Lycra-clad Numpty', or words to that effect. Simon's response? 'Cycle lanes are for Pussies.'

Shortly after, the dual carriageway joined another equally busy road to form a sort of four-lane super-highway. I believe those who don't follow the 'Cycle lanes are for Pussies,' approach to life might consider it a motorway of sorts, and we were stuck in the middle of it. Our road had come from the right and so we were now effectively riding in the third lane, the inside two lanes of traffic, coming from our left-hand side, doing speeds of 70mph or more.

To those of us in the middle of it, riding a bicycle, the vehicles appeared to be moving at the speed of light. Probably the same light we would soon be seeing as we made our way to heaven (if we were lucky). I've often wondered, if such a place exists, do you have to enter in the clothes you were wearing when you left this mortal coil? If so, we would spend the rest of eternity in sweaty cycling gear. It could be worse though. Lycra would be much more uncomfortable if we ended up in the hotter place instead. There, eternity would be like one endless spin class in a small, stuffy studio – with a broken air conditioning unit.

We had to get across to the hard shoulder, to relative safety, but to do so involved pedalling for your life, whilst trying to look over your left shoulder for cars and lorries approaching at breakneck speed, literally. We waited and waited for that small window of opportunity in which to dive across, my fingers pale white from gripping the handlebars so tightly. After what seemed like forever, the moment came.

'Go! Go! Go!' I screamed at Simon, and we put in a burst of acceleration faster than anything so far on the journey, reaching the security of the hard shoulder. I was pumped full of adrenaline. Pedalling became very difficult as I was shaking like I was riding a pneumatic drill, with two tumble dryers for wheels. We reached the roundabout that brought us back to the planned route, then turned right onto a quiet country lane and rode on as if nothing had happened. It was like sailing in becalmed waters after several hours at sea in a hurricane.

'Sorry about that, my bad', said Simon.

'What? Is that it? We nearly died!'

'Yeah, we did. But cycle lanes are still for Pussies.'

He chuckled to himself, and on we rode. He has since accepted that his route choice nearly got us killed and proffered a more complete apology.

What followed was hours of unremarkable riding – through Loughborough, well-known for the accomplishments of its university's sports science department (graduates include Lord Sebastian Coe, Paula Radcliffe MBE, Baroness Tanni Grey-Thompson, Sir Clive Woodward, and numerous other sporting superstars), but not for its natural beauty. Out the other side, we turned to head directly south-west and spent the time stopping and starting, looking at the map trying to find shortcuts down small country lanes to make the day shorter.

The target was home – Redditch, the place I grew up in. We'd planned the route to see family along the way whenever we could, both as a morale booster and a money-saver. Free lodgings and good food, plus a break from another uncomfortable night lying on hard ground separated only by a one-centimetre piece of foam.

Finally, we began to reach places I knew – Fillongley, then Meriden, where I used to train a wonderful 72-year-old lady named Mary. She may have been a pensioner, but she had the spirit, and youthful energy, of a teenager. Meriden was also of special geographical significance – we'd made it to the very centre of England. There was still a long way to go, but we were growing ever more confident that we might pull this off.

I rang ahead to let my folks know our expected ETA and was instructed to head for a pub on the outskirts of town. From here on in, we didn't need a map. I knew the way home. We wound down beautiful country lanes as the light of the day began to fade. Arriving just before complete darkness set in (which was lucky as we had no idea where the bike lights were), we were surprised and delighted to be greeted by a crowd of family and friends.

We spent the evening recounting tales of our adventure so far. We also reminisced about Mike. We talked of our progress with the charity fundraising efforts, having collected almost two thousand pounds so far. I also explained how Simon had tried to kill us earlier that day. It still makes me shudder at the thought.

Simon toasted being alive with a mixture of beer and red wine. It was the first night on the ride that he'd got properly drunk, and I wasn't sure if he were celebrating how far we'd come or settling his nerves after our little detour down the highway. Later, we were even more surprised and delighted to discover that my folks had booked us two rooms in the hotel next door to the pub. Fed, watered, and a little tipsy, we slept the sleep of people who were glad to still be alive.

Chapter 12: An Easy Day with a Hard Finish

Day 9: Monday 3rd September.
Redditch to Minchinhampton Common
(56 miles)

We'd been looking forward to reaching this point since the start. After our longest leg to date yesterday, we now had a couple of shorter days' riding ahead of us. First, we'd be staying with Kirsty's parents in the Cotswolds, and then sleeping in our own beds back home in Bristol, before entering the final leg of the journey down through the South West.

It was only about half a day's riding today, and flat for ninety per cent of it. We followed A-roads much of the way to Cheltenham and, I know I'm repeating myself, but it really is something I would do differently if I had the chance again. A-roads are generally quicker, but they're also largely dull, head down affairs where

91

constant traffic, and the speed at which it goes by, mean you are frequently on edge and rarely get the chance to appreciate your surroundings. Deathly dull is perhaps more accurate.

I don't think I was aware of this as much back then. I felt shielded by the invincibility of youth, and I was very focused on achieving our goal in a set timeframe. This meant covering reasonably long distances each day – something that was made easier by the quicker A-roads.

On the plus side, today's roads were at least flat and most possessed a wide hard shoulder. We rode through the Vale of Evesham, verdant with its numerous fruit farms. The wind didn't seem too bad and we made good time. We skirted past Cheltenham and onto the quieter roads of the Cotswold Hills, home to the rich, famous and royalty. It's a place full of chocolate box villages, tea rooms, babbling brooks, expensive looking cars, and even more expensive houses, built with the distinctive golden limestone quarried from right beneath our wheels.

Kirsty's parents lived in a beautiful house, with an even more beautiful view atop Minchinhampton Common. The problem with it being 'atop' is that to get there, you have to cycle up any one of a wide choice of fairly steep roads. It may surprise you but the roads through Scotland and the north of England had been largely flat or undulating; not many lung-busting hills save for the short sharp slopes of our 'road to hell' experience on the A68, with the biker gangs.

'The W', as it is known locally, climbs out of Nailsworth, up onto the common. Its start is marked by a cattle grid, something that always tells you that you're about to get off the beaten path and will probably have to work hard. I actually enjoyed the climb. My legs felt fresh after a short day with kinder winds, and the hill was at least something different to focus on – as Simon would call it, a 'changement de rythme.' He'd shout this out every time we reached a hill and have to change down into a smaller gear, our cadence quickly adapting as gravity exerted its powerful influence.

He had a seemingly endless supply of these French phrases, each relating to a particular aspect of cycling, and collected through many years of watching the Tour de France. It was like riding with a cross between Del Boy and Bradley Wiggins.

'Allez, allez, allez', came the cry when he wanted us to push on, and he referred to our water bottles as 'bidons'. He termed me his 'domestique,' or in other words, his dogsbody, the rider who does the hard work at the front, so that the team leader (Simon) can take it easy until the final moments of the day. Incidentally, this arrangement has continued to this very day.

We had also developed our own terms. One such shout was 'sit in,' which essentially meant, *this hill looks bloody long – so let's take it easy*. I heard the shout just after the cattle grid, dropped through the gears and took my time, letting my mind wander as we made our way towards the finish for the day.

People often ask me what I think about on the long runs and rides that have become such an integral part of my life.

'Don't you get bored?' they'll say. And the truth is, no, never, not for one second have I ever been bored in all the years of doing these challenges. Tired, yes. In pain, definitely. Low, absolutely. Emotional, angry, upset, nervous, elated, relaxed, determined, absent-minded and without a care in the world – but never bored.

During an event like this one – where you have a partner – sometimes you talk about life, sometimes you talk about what's coming up on the route, at other times you talk about your shared experiences so far, often you just talk plain nonsense. Every now and then, you sense that the other person needs some quiet time, and a peaceful silence descends. Or you might be concerned about your partner, noticing that something has changed in their mood or eating habits.

On some occasions you worry about whether or not you're going to be able to get through the challenge, whilst on others you're simply awestruck by the scenery; feeling on top of the world because of an amazing downhill section, or because you've suddenly had an unexpected surge of energy burst through your veins. Sometimes you're angry because some moron has driven by way too close. Sometimes you're hungry, or thirsty, or working out when you next need to eat or drink. Some of your time is spent navigating, some just trundling along daydreaming about something or other – maybe a trivial work or home matter, planning your next holiday or even your next great adventure.

When you're really finding it hard, that's when you fall back on your coping mechanisms. If you're doing it for a good cause, you might think about the charity, or the loved one you lost that brought you here – to this place and specific moment in time. You think about the good luck messages people sent you, and you think about not wanting to let them down. You use breathing techniques or counting, as I've mentioned previously. You focus in on the bit that hurts and try to get it to relax. You hope that something else will start hurting instead, or sometimes you scream out loud because the pain is so bad. You think about many things, past, present, and future, but you are never, ever, bored.

We arrived at Kirsty's parents' house by mid-afternoon, allowing us plenty of time for rest and recovery. The hours were spent reclining, reading and generally relaxing. Our respite was only interrupted when we had to pop out onto the common to give an interview for local radio. This added an exciting element to the day. It was something different to do, and a good opportunity to promote our cause.

These days such promotions would likely have had a bigger impact – because people can get online and donate in a matter of seconds. Back then, we were still getting people to sponsor us on paper forms, promising to give a certain amount of money when the challenge had been completed. There was something about the old way that I rather liked. You had to earn your sponsorship money. Don't get me wrong, online sponsorship sites are much slicker and, most importantly, get the money to the charity a lot quicker, albeit in many cases for a fee. But, I've always liked the idea of having to push myself so that people felt like they were getting value for money from me. It felt more like a binding contract between us. They had to sign the form in person, committing to a certain amount in advance, and I had to commit to getting the challenge done. The disadvantage back then, of course, was that you had to chase people up for the money afterwards, which often took months and some people you just never saw again.

I don't think that all charity events have to be gruelling punishment, but I do think people should ideally have to do something that takes them out of their comfort zone, relative to their fitness or abilities. Charity is omnipresent these days and I think it's sad that it's just become expected of people to give. Most people don't have much spare cash and they're so frequently asked to part with it for a good cause. There are a huge number of worthy causes and, without this kind of help, many would not be able to do the amazing things they do.

It does make you question, though, how well the nation is served by its Government, when so many seemingly essential services rely on people's kindness, giving money they could often do with themselves? I guess that's another reason why I always feel that, if I am going to ask for sponsorship, the challenge needs to be even bigger, even harder than the last one. I can tell you for certain, nine days into this one, we really felt like we were earning our sponsorship.

Chapter 13: Niagara Falls

Day 10: Tuesday 4th September.
Minchinhampton Common to Bristol (33 miles)

Today was different for a number of reasons. Firstly, we were now firmly in familiar territory. It was just over 30 miles to our respective homes in Bristol, and so we were in for a much shorter and easier day. Secondly, Simon's friend, Rob, would be joining us for the remaining 250 miles to Land's End. This gave the ride a very different atmosphere, but thankfully not in a bad way. It felt like a mini adventure within an adventure. Rob was a welcome addition to the crew, largely because he could sit at the front and take the brunt of the wind, which was, once more, strongly against us.

I was actually starting to feel fitter as the ride went on, but Simon was beginning each day more and more fatigued. It likely had a lot to do with our evening routines. We both focused on carb-loading – to top up our glycogen stores (the body's stored form of carbohydrates) – but Simon was supplementing it with a few cigarettes and occasionally alcohol too.

Yes, Simon's recovery routines could have been a little better. What I haven't said, though, is how much I relied on him throughout the ride. I have massive respect for people who take on challenges of this nature on their own.

An expedition partner provides you with practical support in so many ways. For instance, when it comes to taking turns at the front – to shelter you from the wind for a while – or fixing problems with your bike (something that, amazingly, we hadn't had to do since my second puncture way back on the banks of Loch Lochy – a week previously). They provide entertainment and, most important of all, understanding. They can see, hear, and even sense when you're finding things tough, and they learn how best to deal with this. Maybe by offering you a drink or energy bar; spending longer on their stint at the front; offering words of support or, conversely, a little tough love when needed; or even just giving you a little bit of space. It's amazing how refreshing it can be just to have 10 metres or so between you for a while. It's a great way to overcome cabin fever (or I suppose in this case, saddle fever).

In the years since this ride, Simon has become like a brother to me. We have completed many more adventures (I'll be writing about them in future books) and come to really know each other's ways – our strengths and weaknesses, and the merits and pitfalls of our characters. In time, I have also learned things that helped me to understand why Simon is like he is, and he me.

Not that many years before we met, his brother had committed suicide and this, as you can obviously imagine, had placed a huge strain on Simon and his parents. He'll tell you himself that it took much of his 20s and well into his 30s to learn to cope with his grief. Until he found a better way, this often came from the textbook, *How Not to Deal With Stuff*, co-written by Paul Gascoigne and Amy Winehouse.

At least his drinking escapades often provided amusing stories. Like the time he broke his wrist falling off a jacuzzi, or broke his fingers whilst trying to catch me out playing cricket, or when he was run over by a taxi, breaking the windscreen with his forehead. On this last occasion the taxi driver followed Simon to the hospital, and into the A&E department, where he told him in no uncertain terms that he must pay for a new windscreen – having wilfully damaged the original by choosing to somersault up over the bonnet and headbutt it.

Our John o' Groats to Land's End adventure became a huge turning point in Simon's life. His level of training and fitness sky-rocketed in subsequent years, and yet he is still somehow able to stop for a pint or two after a hundred-mile stint and head off 'refuelled,' at a staggering pace. Having been there for each other through good times and bad, I am confident that he won't be at all offended by my description of our journey. We'll probably have a good laugh about it whilst he has a glass of red wine and I enjoy a pomegranate juice.

Now three musketeers, with Rob, we set off across the common, descended 'The W', and turned south onto the A46. Another fast, busy stretch of road, it was the flattest way to get to Bristol and we moved along at good speed for a couple of miles until Rob punctured. We'd ridden nigh on 500 miles without incident, and here we were about ten minutes into our new team set-up, having to stop for repairs. Over the next hour we endured further stops for punctures and chain issues. These things happen of course, but I could tell Simon was irked by the situation as we were unable to get into our usual rhythm.

Eventually the A46 crossed the M4 and we began the hair-raising descent towards the Roman town of Bath. These days, I would never dream of riding that stretch of highway, with its winding road and huge volume of traffic moving along at ridiculous speeds. Short of the spa town, we turned west for Bristol and finished with a much more pleasant ride into the centre, along the former Bristol to Bath railway line. It was the first stretch of track, axed by Beeching in the 60s, to be converted into a purpose-built cycleway – in 1979 – by the cycling and sustainable transport charity, *Sustrans*.

There are now hundreds of miles of cycle paths built along former railway lines all over Britain, but the charity still has its HQ in Bristol city centre, and it felt highly appropriate that we should be riding this stretch as part of our adventure. I probably take the line for granted these days, having ridden it on so many occasions, but it truly is a wonder. Along the way are dotted sculptures marking the industrial heritage of the route, old platforms, and stations, some of which have been turned into pleasant cafes and tea rooms, thick forests, small stone cottages and grand manor houses. The River Avon snakes underneath every few miles, and provides a range of pubs with gardens perfect for refreshment stops on sunnier days. On part of the route, there is even a steam railway with regular trains and a lovely little museum. If you've never had the pleasure of riding it, I strongly advise you to give it a try.

We were met by the girls in the city centre and headed off to our separate homes for a night of familiarity and rest, or rather, we would have if a rather large spanner hadn't been thrown into the works. Bek and I pulled into the driveway of our pleasant little semi-detached and opened the front door, ready to begin unloading the bike and bags. The door led into a tiny little square hallway, no more than a few feet in each direction, before heading straight up the stairs or into the lounge through another doorway to the left. Bek noticed that the carpet in the hallway was surprisingly wet, and when she opened the door to the lounge, we were met with a sight that filled us with sheer horror.

I can only describe it as a sort of indoor Niagara Falls. It looked as if it may have been put together by Tracy Emin to convey some ironic message about modern living. Much of the ceiling had collapsed, leaving just the edges of the upstairs bedroom and a gigantic hole in the centre. Through this hole an endless stream of water poured onto the sofa and then everything else in the room. The bed had fallen through and was resting on top of the TV, at a rather jaunty angle. Many items of bedroom furniture had joined it, along with plaster and debris from the ceiling. It appeared as if the house had been struck by a stray North Korean missile – or maybe Kim Jong-il felt the North Bristol suburb of Brentry was a target of strategic significance, in which case he'd been mightily ill-advised.

Upon investigation, I discovered that the leak appeared to be coming from the hot water tank in the cupboard on the landing. Not being technically minded, I had no idea why, and to be honest, it didn't really matter. All I needed to know was that it was very wet, and that we could not stay there. We switched off the water and electricity supply, then retreated to the relative safety of the driveway, where we began making calls – firstly to the insurance company, then to Kirsty and Simon, requesting the use of their sofa bed for the evening. They obliged, of course, but secretly I think they were hoping (as we had been) for a little time to themselves. Still, we had a good laugh about it over dinner whilst Simon polished off a bottle of Cabernet Sauvignon.

Chapter 14: "Die, Roadies"

Day 11: Wednesday 5th September.
Bristol to Crediton (85 miles)

You could be forgiven for thinking that our flood disaster might have spelt the end of our journey, but we'd come so far and, in relative terms, were so close to the finish, that we were not going to let a newly installed indoor water feature put paid to our dreams. An added incentive was that we didn't have anywhere to live, that didn't currently look like a very run-down water park so, after further phone calls to the insurance company, on we went.

Out of Bristol, more A-roads swept us into the South West proper. Due to a road closure, we were forced into a small diversion towards Weston-Super-Mare. Translated from its Latin roots, the town's name means, 'Weston above sea.' Like many British seaside towns, it had its heyday in the Victorian era, with people from Bristol and the Midlands flooding in by train, and others by paddle steamer from South Wales.

Weston's halcyon days may be long gone, but you'll still hear the familiar Bristolian, Welsh, and Brummie accents all along the promenade today. Families still head to the beach for fun and sunbathing, to the pier for fairground rides, or to the numerous arcades where inflation has turned the 2p slot machines of my childhood memories into 10p machines with £20 notes as prizes.

As a child, I spent many happy family holidays at the seaside, playing for hours on the slot machines (a pastime that has somehow miraculously earned itself its own gameshow in the form of ITV's Tipping Point), building sandcastles, playing crazy golf, eating fish and chips, or watching Punch and Judy shows. I think there's real joy to be found at the British seaside. The arcades, with their bright lights, music, and ingenious mechanics, are I suppose the great grandparents of our modern-day mobile phones and games consoles.

There are also the huge health and wellbeing benefits to be gained from a visit to the seaside. We know that the sight and sound of water has a positive impact on our mood, and people have been writing about the bracing effects of the sea air for centuries. The fresh, cold breeze somehow makes everything seem so much clearer and, the gentle lapping of the waves in such sharp contrast to the shrill cries of the seagulls, all serve to make us feel thoroughly wonderful.

We made it past Brent Knoll, the flat-topped hill and former iron-age settlement that you can see on your right when driving south down the M5. It's a steep climb, but well worth the small diversion to walk to the top if you have the time to spare. You'll be rewarded with 360-degree views out into the Bristol Channel and across to Wales to the West, South West over the Somerset Levels, and East to the Mendip Hills. The deep cut of Cheddar Gorge – the ice-age formation and largest gorge in England – is just visible in the distance. Heading deeper into Somerset, the route became fairly dull. We followed the A38 through the towns of Bridgwater and Taunton, before crossing into the county of Devon and down to Tiverton.

Nothing much happened. We pedalled, cars went by, we occasionally stopped for snacks, we pedalled some more. The A-road journey was once again proving mundane and, by this point, Simon was tired. He had failed to recover from last night's Liam Gallagher-style diet of cigarettes and alcohol. Although on most evenings he'd only had one or two beers and a few cigarettes, this plus a couple of heavy nights in Redditch and Bristol had begun to take its toll. I have to point this out because, when he saw the first draft of this book, Simon felt like it read as if I were cycling around Britain with Father Jack from the TV series Father Ted. Whilst earlier I said that he is somewhat like an ethanol-powered bus, even he couldn't ride from John o' Groats to Land's End on an endless diet of booze and fags. Rob had asthma and sometimes needed to stop to use his inhalers. It made the ride challenging at times for him too.

Simon spent much of the last part of the ride in silence, at the rear of our small peloton. After stops where we'd take a combination of Lucozade, coffee, and Nurofen – something we termed 'Rocket Fuel' – he would undergo a terrifying transformation. As I rode along, all I could hear behind me were weird grunts, yelps, and other strange, indescribable noises.

My imagination brought forth images of his Lycra being torn at the seams, as a large, despicable, hairy creature burst through. I never looked back. Not just through fear, but because turning my head was nigh-on impossible on such busy roads.

The fearful image of the monster I had in my head, though, was nothing compared to what I was forced to witness when I did have to ride behind Simon. His incredibly see-through cycling shorts offered me a view I never want to see again; one I suspect I am cursed to live with to my dying day. And so, I did a lot of work at the front, grinding the pedals around as we toiled into the incessant headwind. These days, it's Simon who's much the stronger rider, and so I often sit on his wheel. Thankfully, he also now has much better shorts.

At Tiverton we finally escaped the busy A-roads and headed south. It being Devon, steep, round-topped green hills rose on either side of us but, luckily, we seemed to be following the path of a river. Up ahead to the right we could see a monstrous-looking green eminence. Things seemed to be going our way as the road curved left. Simon prematurely shouted with glee.

'Looks like we're in luck lads.'

But before his whoops and hollers had died away, the route we needed turned sharply back to the right, away from the main road that frustratingly crossed a beautiful stone bridge and continued to wind its way easily down the valley. We began to climb.

It was at this point I discovered I had a problem with my gears. A problem in the sense that I now appeared to have only one – they wouldn't change. The Airborne had served me so well thus far, that a hitch this close to the end seemed almost inevitable. I've never been particularly knowledgeable about bike mechanics. Even now, when we organise cycling events, I bring someone along who has the necessary skills to keep everyone moving. Back then my abilities were limited to pumping up a tyre, changing an inner tube, and knowing that if anything else was required, I needed help.

I did what I could, which was to angrily press the gear levers until the chain ground its way into the smallest gear it would reach, and I slogged my way to the top of the hill, legs moving as if in fast-setting cement. Near the top I caught the others, as the incline levelled out enough to be suitable for the gear in which I'd found myself, and we rode through one of those wondrous natural tunnels you get in the English countryside. The branches from trees, on both sides of the road, leant over to form a verdant roof through which dappled sunlight shone down. It was like cycling into heaven – serene and beautiful.

That peace didn't last long. We saw a car approaching, the first for some time and, as it drew nearer, it appeared that the man driving it was naked, certainly on his top half, at any rate. Nearer still and I could see that he was drinking a can of beer. As he passed us, he threw the can out of his window in our direction, whilst shouting, 'Die, roadies!'

Simon's parents lived just a few miles away, and he assured us that this was pretty standard behaviour for these parts. On we pedalled, dropping down into the town of Crediton for the rendezvous with the girls and his family. Bek and Kirsty were now enjoying their fourth night in a row without having to pitch the tent, a fact that had definitely helped to ease the tensions in the group. They deserved a rest given what they'd had to endure to get us here.

We spent a beautiful evening in Simon's parents' cottage on the edge of Dartmoor, before sleeping in the most wonderful wooden outhouse. It was a cross between a summerhouse and a log cabin, situated at the end of their garden. It was a great place to just sit outside, look up and enjoy the brilliantly starry skies, so clear due to the lack of cloud cover and the rural location on the edge of the moor. Thinking about just how far away the faint twinkling lights above our heads were made our journey feel very small indeed. We had just two days and over 100 miles to go now. That felt well within our reach.

Chapter 15: Ups and Downs

Day 12: Thursday 6th September.
Crediton to Bodmin (64 miles).

Before we could begin today's ride, we had to get the Airborne's gears sorted. Remarkably, after all this way, the only mechanical problems we'd had were my punctures on days one and two, and Rob's numerous issues on the first morning that he'd joined us. We found a shop, explained we were on an end-to-end adventure, and that time was of the essence. The shop was based just off the main route to Cornwall, so I'm pretty certain they'd heard similar stories countless times before. However, they kindly fixed the gears on the spot and we were once more on our way, still headed for the end of the British mainland.

We were soon on the A30, another lethal A-road, with a constant stream of cars, vans and lorries flying by. It's the most direct route to Land's End, but it is no fun and, if I were to do it again, I'd have absolutely no hesitation in trading it for quieter roads, even if it meant steeper hills. In fact, it was so unpleasant that I'd have happily ridden along the soft sandy beaches instead, even with the tide in.

We pressed on, up onto Bodmin Moor, through a moonscape even bleaker than our first day's riding out of John o' Groats. After passing the famous hilltop Jamaica Inn, the setting for Daphne du Maurier's 1936 novel of the same name, we paused for a lunchtime catch-up in a layby with the girls. To call it a layby is to do it a disservice – not many British laybys have the kind of spectacular panorama this one did. In every direction, views of the Moor's barren heathland, with its dark foreboding lakes and rocky outcrops, stretched to the horizon.

We dropped down into the town of Bodmin, our final overnight stop before the grand finale the next day. There was exhaustion but there was also a sense of excitement, an unwavering belief now that we were going to do it, save for some major misfortune. Tomorrow wasn't a long ride in the grand scheme – only 60 miles or so. We'd ridden nigh on 900 miles already, averaging about 75 miles every day. We thought it quite an achievement for complete novices in the art of long-distance cycling.

I was pretty sure that Simon was looking forward to it being over, and I knew for definite that the girls were, but there was a small part of me that just wanted to keep going. This was the first time that I realised how much I thrive on the buzz of adventures like these. Marathons are different of course. The constant pounding of the pavement means that, towards the end, you're simply clinging on and praying for the finish line. But all of these days in the saddle had given me an appetite for more.

For me, the beauty of cycling lies in how much you feel like you belong to the scenery as you journey through it. You have time to really appreciate your surroundings. It's not like being in a car, where the scenery is simply a blur out of the window.

Back on day one, when it felt like we would never make it, I couldn't wait to get those oil rigs out of my sight. Increasingly, though, the journey had given me a great sense of the rewards you reap through patience. Keep moving those pedals, one turn at a time, and you'll eventually get to where you're headed. Yes, my legs felt tired but, as I said before, the fatigue was never linear. It ebbed and flowed like the tide. Sometimes the going felt extremely tough but then, all of a sudden and for no apparent reason, my energy would return, and I'd be flying.

The other thing I was learning about cycling was that the more time you spend on your bike, the more you felt at one with it. It becomes like another limb, an extension of you. I'd grown to understand the Airborne well. I knew its capabilities in braking, accelerating, and turning, and could now move it about effortlessly, with a small shift of my bodyweight. A far cry from my first training ride over the Mendip Hills, when I'd felt like I was fighting it, when there weren't enough gears, and it all just seemed so hard.

I drifted into sleep with thoughts of continuing our journey still running through my mind. What if we just turned around at Land's End and went back the other way? We should have the wind behind us, or would a freak change in the weather see us battling headwinds all the way up as well as down?

This actually happened many years later when we attempted our Three Peaks challenge: climbing the famous mountains and then cycling the distance in between each. We began at Snowdon, expecting a nice tailwind would push us along as we headed for Scafell Pike and then Ben Nevis. It never did. Instead, we rode for 450 miles north into powerful headwinds.

However, I'm getting ahead of myself. We still had one day to go, but the omens looked good! Our end goal was within pedalling distance.

Chapter 16: The Last First and Last

Day 13: Friday 7th September.
Bodmin to Land's End (56 miles)

We were in no rush to get away. The weather seemed fair, and the distance for our final day was much shorter than we were used to. After a leisurely breakfast, we set off. Bek and Kirsty stayed behind to pack down for the final time. They were now very kindly taking down not just our tent, but Rob's two-man shelter as well. Thankfully there had been no further team issues since everything had exploded in Doncaster. The air seemed to have been cleared by that particular eruption.

We really were a good team by this point, regardless of the rather one-sided division of labour. I think it had probably become easier for the girls the further south we rode. We were closer to home, the weather had improved, and there were less of the daily chores remaining, so it made sense. But (and this was the same for us) it was partly down to getting used to the routines and getting better at managing them. On our side, I think we grew increasingly appreciative of Bek and Kirsty's efforts as the journey wore on, and realised that we definitely had the better half of the deal. We resolved to make it up to them once we were back home. If we could just manage to keep a lid on things for one more day.

We headed straight back onto the A30 but, thankfully, it became less busy, and the passing traffic slower, the further south-west we headed. It was actually reasonably quiet – school had started again, the tourists had gone, and it made for much more pleasant riding. The sun was out for our final day and we took it steady, knowing that we had time to spare and it was simply about the three of us getting to the end in one piece or, more accurately I suppose, in three pieces. We also knew we had an arrival party waiting for us – a number of our friends had headed down from Bristol to cheer us over the finish line, and we were all going to spend the weekend camping in St Ives.

As it turned out, there were no last-minute dramas, no bike issues, no road incidents, no navigation problems. Nothing to deal with save for the pleasant scenery Cornwall had to offer. There was one final obstacle though. One we were unable to pass without stopping. As we drew to within a few miles of the finish, we reached another pub called 'The First and Last.' It seemed like such a long time ago that we'd visited its twin sister, shortly after crossing the border from

Scotland. This time we knew we hadn't missed our turning, and there were no cast members from Alan Partridge serving behind the bar. Instead, the September sun beat down on the little garden as we sat, enjoying a beer (even me), pausing to appreciate the enormity of what we'd done, and savour our achievements before we were surrounded by friends. It's not often you get to do this. No one has a cheeky pint a mile out from the finish of a marathon, you simply slog on until it's done. Rob was also delighted. His journey from the top of the Cotswolds was still a substantial one and he'd ridden strongly.

I'm not sure how long we sat in that beer garden, but it was long enough to start getting phone-calls from the girls asking where we were. Eventually, reluctantly, partly from tired limbs and partly from the realisation that next time we got off our bikes, it would all be over, we sidled back out onto the road. It wasn't just me now – we were all a little sad at this thought. It's strange how you don't want something that had, at times, been so tiring, so uncomfortable, so painful, and so mentally taxing, to end. There's an adrenaline that keeps you driving towards the completion of your mission and it becomes quite addictive.

Back on the road, we had just one mile to go. One last chance to turn the pedals, to look up and take in the scenery. The green, rolling landscape dotted with rocky outcrops, old stone buildings, bright yellow gorse and, for the first time on the horizon, the faint change in the shade of blue where sea met sky. One last time we sang 'Lidl by Lidl,' and then we saw the stone markers by the side of the road – 'Welcome to Land's End,' they said. Up ahead we could see the large car park with the bright white visitor's centre beyond, fronted by palatial columns. It was an odd architectural mishmash of fisherman's cottage and ancient Greece.

Riding into the car park, we were greeted by a sea of orange, white, and blue balloons provided by our charities – the National Society for Epilepsy and Cancer Research. There was also a sea of people. Bek and Kirsty of course, to whom we are eternally grateful for allowing us to follow our dream. The girls had been joined by our friends from Bristol - Alan and Sam, Dave and Erica, Tom and Lindsay, Gilly and Amy, and Rob's wife, Tania. And beyond them, just the sea itself or, more correctly, the Atlantic Ocean.

It was a wonderful feeling to be cheered over that finish line, providing one final surge of adrenaline. It's hard to describe the elation you experience when you complete a big adventure such as this. There's the exhilaration at the successful completion of your mission, mixed with an equal measure of relief that it's finally over. There's also a feeling of pride in yourself for overcoming all of the hurdles along the way. For us, these had included punctures, navigational challenges, near-death experiences with motorbikes and on four-lane superhighways, hunger, pain, almost constant hills to conquer, and endless headwinds to battle. I was proud of raising money for a great cause, but sad thinking about lost friends. I welled up. It was not just the huge mix of emotions but also, I suspect, the emotional instability that comes from exhaustion.

Then there were hugs, handshakes, high fives, photographs, and time spent recounting our adventures. The sun shone brightly and, whilst it remained breezy, it felt warm – a far cry from the conditions when we'd set off from John o' Groats almost a fortnight ago. We headed to the famous sign for one final photograph, just to prove that it really happened. We had to pay for this one, but it was worth it to commemorate our achievements. The picture still sits on the windowsill in my lounge. I'm looking at it now as I write. We look pretty chuffed with ourselves, and we're wearing far fewer layers than we were in the photograph at the start.

We weren't the fastest, we hadn't done it on unicycles, Penny Farthings, or while hitting a golf ball all the way. In fact, there was nothing particularly special about our journey, save for the fact that it was ours and ours alone. In that sense, each and every Land's End to John o' Groats journey is unique, and made no less special because others have gone before and done it quicker or in quirkier ways. It wasn't, I realised, about being the best, but rather being your best.

Simon and I embraced and congratulated each other. In that moment, our lifelong friendship was set. We made a great team. When I got the opportunity, whilst others were chatting and eating ice creams, I slipped away and walked my bike to the rear of the hotel. I stood looking down at the jumble of rocks that led down to the crashing waves of the sea, and thought to myself, it really is all downhill from here.

Chapter 17: Lines in the Sand

My memory of our celebratory weekend is a little blurred. We had the most wonderful time camping in the sand dunes. Relaxing in the daytime, and making campfires on the beach at night, toasting marshmallows, and drinking – there was definitely a fair bit of that. I suspect it was the main reason why my recollection of events is so hazy. There were occasional fallouts too. One member of our party (they shall remain nameless) decided to retire early to sleep one night, only to be kept awake by the drunken chatter and silliness outside – tents aren't particularly good at keeping noise out. We all got a stern telling off, but it didn't matter.

One moment on the Saturday night does stand out in my memory. As the sun fell and the tide started to come in, we all stood together, drawing a line in the sand with a stick – at the point that the waves reached as they rolled up the beach. The aim of the game was to stand firm without getting your feet wet. As each round of waves slithered their way towards us, we all shouted, 'hold the line!' as loudly as we could. It was a game of chicken with the North Atlantic Ocean. Futile – of course – but rendered hilarious by copious amounts of alcohol and the wonderful camaraderie within the group. Each time the waves came in that little bit further, and we were forced to retreat, running away in true *Monty Python and the Holy Grail* style, but it was great fun, nonetheless. Looking back, it feels like maybe this was the moment when we drew a line (imaginary though it was) under our great adventure.

The next day we all had pretty sore heads. I'm sure you can guess who had the sorest. By late morning, there was still no sign of Simon, and we had to take the tents down and begin the long journey home. Kirsty had no joy in trying to rouse him from his sleeping bag where he was cocooned like a turtle that had retreated into its shell.

We sent in the cavalry. Simon is terrified of our friend Erica – she does the angry and disappointed look very well. He will usually do as he is told after a stern ticking off from her. When even her warnings went unheeded, we simply decided to dismantle the tent around him. It probably was the hangover, but I did wonder whether he just wanted to cling on to the adventure for as long as possible.

Things returned to normal. We headed back to work and the mundanity of day-to-day life. After the elation of the moment has subsided, there follows a void, an emptiness. You can lack motivation to do any training for a while because, well, there's nothing to train for. In fact, you can lack the motivation to do much at all. It's an extreme form of post-holiday blues. Thankfully, this feeling diminishes as your energy levels return. You begin to exercise again and, once more, become accustomed to the routine of everyday existence.

One day, a few years later, the inspiration for the next big adventure hit me like a bolt from the blue. I texted Simon:

'Fancy a trip to the pub?'

'Yeah sure. Why not?' he replied.

'I've got an idea for our next challenge.'

'Oh. Should I tell Kirsty?'

'Hmm. Not just yet, no. Not just yet.'

Part 2: How to Have Your Own End-to-End Adventure

Chapter 18: Taking on LeJog and Other Long-Distance Rides

In this chapter, I've included all the things we learned during the planning and execution of our JogLe ride, and our other long-distance challenges to date. Since 2007, the world of technology has changed significantly, so I've included mention of innovations that weren't available to us at the time and which should make your adventure much simpler. You'll find advice on everything you need – including on plotting your route, training, nutrition, equipment choices, mental coping mechanisms – for when the going gets tough – and other tips to make the days run smoothly. Much of this advice is not specific to LeJog. It can be useful in planning any long-distance ride.

It's also worth mentioning the things I have not included. I have not created a day-by-day training plan. In my 20 years of experience as a personal trainer, I have learned that each person's preparation for an event like this is unique and should be based on factors like their available time, fitness level, previous injuries, sleep patterns, exercise preferences, and much more besides.

Instead, I have outlined key targets that you can aim for which will help you prepare for the ride.

I have also not gone into the detail of heart rate training zones or using power meters to target specific Wattage: you don't need to be a high-level athlete or have fancy kit to take on this challenge. You may well be taking it on primarily for the experience and to see the sights our beautiful land has to offer. I have, though, provided some simple techniques for gauging the intensity of your training, and some suggestions of interval sessions which will help increase your fitness for the ride.

Finally, there is no detailed discussion here of the technical aspects of cycling like gear ratios, or specific bike components. Bicycle gearing is mentioned briefly for those of you with no idea about how it works and what you may require, but there is such a vast array of options that this is something you'll probably need to discuss in more detail with your local bike mechanic. And if you're a cycling enthusiast, you'll likely know much more than I do about bike mechanics, so I'm confident you can make your own choices on gears and other bike parts.

Let it be said now, something will almost certainly go wrong along the route. Punctures, mechanical failures, aches and pains, freak weather conditions, navigational issues – you'd be unlucky if all of these occurred on your ride, but don't be surprised if you experience one or more of them. Expect it, prepare for it as best you can and then learn to take the rough with the smooth. It is a challenge after all – you wouldn't want it to be too easy, would you? Without the hiccups and disasters, where are the tales and stories to bring out in the pub, at the dinner table, and in your own book should you be so inclined? Chances are, whatever goes wrong will be dwarfed, in retrospect, by what goes right. Hold onto that thought when you're lost and battling into a vicious headwind.

One final point to make – I am not connected to or paid by any of the companies or organisations mentioned here. I have simply listed some resources that you may find useful. It goes without saying that alternatives to most of them are available. It's up to you to decide what's best for your needs.

18.1 Route Planning

Firstly, ask yourself two questions: 'How much work do I want to do in terms of route planning?' and 'How much help do I want along the way?' This will help you choose between the following options:

Joining an Organised Ride

If you want to do little or no planning, and get as much help as possible, get yourself online and check out the numerous companies that do organised 'End-to-End' trips. There you'll find a range of packages, from pre-planned routes and organised overnight stays, right through to full vehicle support, meals, and sometimes even guide riders. You'll have to pay for them, of course, but it'll remove the difficulties of organising your adventure, leaving you to focus solely on training and enjoying the ride. Probably the largest event is the *Deloitte Ride Across Britain*, but you'll find packages through *CTC Cycling Holidays*, a wide range of options through the ever-useful *Cycle: End to End* website (cycle-endtoend.org.uk), and plenty more by simply carrying out an internet search.

Using a Pre-planned Route

If you want to take a little more responsibility for your adventure, while still following a pre-planned route, the *Cycling UK* website has free downloadable PDF guides and GPX files (the ones you load into a GPS device like a Garmin, for example), plus articles and a chat forum. They have three routes on offer, all taking around a fortnight: a main road route to get you there quickly, or B&B and youth hostel-based routes to make it easy to plan your accommodation along the way.

The cycling charity *Sustrans* has a purchasable guidebook complete with maps. It'll take you on a longer route, utilising the *National Cycle Network* (a huge inter-connecting system of on-road and off-road cycling routes) and quiet country lanes wherever possible. Whilst it adds a couple of hundred miles to the journey, they break it up into 28 sections, making for a pleasant daily average of 43 miles over four weeks. You can of course choose to do it faster (or slower).

A range of route cards providing different options are purchasable from the *Cycle End to End* website mentioned in the organised rides section, and there's also a Cicerone guide compiled by Nick Mitchell, a highly experienced cyclist and 'End-to-End' rider, plus plenty of other books and websites each with their own take on the route.

Planning Your Own Route

For me, the joy of an adventure comes from making it truly my own, and that means planning the route myself. By taking full responsibility, I feel like I own it and it is uniquely mine. That's why I will always choose this option, but that choice comes from experience. If you opt to plan your own route, you should be aware that organising a trip of this distance takes a fair amount of time. You'll most likely work your way through a number of versions and experience more than a little frustration along the way. There are a huge number of choices available to you – in terms of both route options and the tools with which you plan the journey. Here are some hints and tips to help make it easier.

1.   Even if planning your own route, check out a few pre-made ones first, to get some idea of commonly ridden paths and great things to see along the way.

2.   Take a look at the *National Cycle Network* on the *Sustrans* Website. You can use the network as the foundation for your route, and then add in places of interest or trips to see family and friends along the way. They've recently linked up with *Ordnance Survey* to produce an interactive map. This enables you to see which sections are on-road (purple) or off-road (yellow). You can also click on a route to get more information (details about the types of surface you'll encounter, route guidance and things to see and do), and download some sections as a GPX file.

3.   Think carefully about the types of roads (or paths) you wish to follow. If you are time-limited, or you want to push yourself to do the journey in ten days or less, you'll likely spend more time on main roads – they are generally less hilly and more direct. If not, my advice (and hopefully the conclusion you'll have come to by reading this book) is to go for quieter road options wherever possible. This ride is a once-in-a-lifetime opportunity for most people and, in my humble opinion, it's a huge shame if you spend much of it worrying about the traffic and your general safety. Do bear one thing in mind though. Quieter routes using smaller roads will often mean more hills. You can go one step further and choose to head off-

road completely, following the yellow *Sustrans* routes, or even go wild and hit the bridleways you'll find on detailed OS maps. This will guarantee traffic-free riding, but you'll need to make sure you have the right bike and tyres for it, and be prepared to go much slower. The Great North Trail from *Cycling UK* now offers the chance to ride from the Peak District to John o' Groats entirely off road (on a mountain bike), and there are plans to add a Great South Trail to take you all the way to Land's End.

If you are planning your own route, here are some of the tools available to help you do it:

• *Strava* – the most well-known app. You can plot routes in great detail and then upload them to GPS devices to follow. Don't expect to just type in 'Land's End to John o' Groats' though. You'll be best off checking the route in detail to iron out any glitches and tailoring it to suit you. Sometimes it seems to follow recognised cycle paths, that wiggle all around towns, when you could have just jumped on a road for a few hundred metres. Also check out great features like Heat Maps to show you the most popular routes in an area. There are free and subscription options. As of 2020, many of the key features are part of the subscription package.

• *Komoot* – a pretty impressive alternative to *Strava,*

with free route planning plus, for a one-off fee, a range of cool extra features like voice navigation (effectively turning the app into a GPS) and downloadable maps, so you don't need a GPS signal to use them. There's good detail about the surface you'll be riding, and you can search for campsites, parks, train stations or whatever you're looking for on route. It works with your GPS device too.

• *Cyclestreets.net* – an impressive route planner from a not-for-profit organisation. It gives lots of cool detail and offers a choice of fastest, quietest, or a balanced route (I was particularly pleased with that one). It also tells you how many traffic lights and stops you'll encounter – plus how much CO_2 you'll offset by making the journey by bike – and you can search for cafes, bike shops, railway stations and more. Routes are downloadable as GPX files too.

• *Bikemap.net* – a detailed map with downloadable GPS files and more features in the paid version.

My advice is to try them all out and see which you prefer. Whilst they're similar in some ways, each has a unique user experience, and display their maps slightly differently.

There are plenty of options for GPS devices too. I create my routes on Strava and upload them as GPX files to a Garmin for navigation, but Wahoo, Lezyne and Polar all offer a range of models. You don't necessarily need a GPS device. You can navigate via your phone using Strava or one of the other apps mentioned previously (even Google has a bike route option these days), but my experience is that doing this drains the battery very quickly and, unless you have an unlimited internet plan, it can also use up your data allowance in record time. If you are going to navigate by phone, be sure to get yourself a good portable power bank for charging. Most devices will fit in a bag on the top tube of your bike. That way you can plug in and power your phone whilst riding. There are many portable batteries on the market. Look for ones that are light and have the highest Milliamp Hours (mAh) – the bigger the number, the longer the battery life. I use one that has 27,000mAh.

Getting to the Start (and Home Again)

If you're participating in an organised ride, they will give you details of where you need to be, and when. All you need to work out is how to get to the meeting point.

If you are planning your own End-to-End ride, you'll need to consider how you get everything (and everyone), to your starting point. The camper van option, whilst not the cheapest, probably affords you the simplest means of doing this. Hire one and you and your support crew can head to the start together, stay in a local campsite overnight, and set off next morning.

Make sure you pre-book your pitches as sites can get extremely busy in the summer months, particularly in Cornwall and the National Park regions. If you're using a car instead, I'd suggest a dry run, well in advance, to ensure that you can fit everything in (including of course, bikes and riders).

Solo cyclists will need to use public transport, or likely face an incredibly long warm-up and cool-down. Penzance is the nearest railway station to Land's End, around 12 miles away. At the other end, Wick is closest to John o' Groats – at 16 miles away – whilst Thurso is only four miles further. You might wish to choose a station that isn't on your route, then you'll get to take in some different scenery and won't feel like you're repeating miles (many JogLe End-to-Enders head south from the start passing Wick, whilst others head west across the top of Scotland through Thurso, before turning south). If you don't wish to cycle extra miles, you could pre-book a taxi to take you from the station to the start line, and vice versa at the finish. Don't just turn up and expect there'll be one waiting that's big enough to fit you and all your gear.

Be aware that, these days, you'll probably need to pre-book your train ticket and reserve a space for your bike. It astonishes me that today's trains have as few as 2-3 available bike spaces. When climate change is such a massive issue, surely it would be common sense to link up greener forms of transport, and make it easier for people to ditch their cars. Instead, my own experience of taking a bike on a train is that you are treated with disdain and much tutting, as if you had asked to stable your camel for the journey.

Be sure to pre-book your homebound tickets too. You're unlikely to want to do more cycling after finishing your ride. If you're not confident on exact arrival dates, aim to do this a few days before you're due to finish, when you have a clearer timeline to work towards. Check out *Plus Bike* by National Rail for information about reservations, taking bikes on trains and more.

18.2 Accommodation

If you're planning your own route, you'll have to ensure that each day's route finishes at your overnight stay (or nearby if using support crew). If you do need to book places to stay along your route, bear the following in mind:

- Pre-book – you don't want to be rocking up late in the day, tired and hungry, only to discover there's no room at the Inn (especially if COVID is still an issue when you take on your challenge).
- Remember that the *Cycling UK, Sustrans,* and *Cicerone* guides offer advice on places to stay along their routes.
- If you really want to rough it, wild camping is

permitted in Scotland (be sure to familiarise yourself with the Scottish Outdoor Access Code beforehand), but you'd need to seek the landowner's permission throughout most of England and Wales. You can wild camp on Dartmoor, but need to check availability in advance with the military, because they use the moor as a live firing range!

- Even if you're using support crew, try to find places as close to (if not directly on) your route as possible. We know from experience that even a commute of half an hour at the start or end of a day can feel frustrating. In the evening you want to eat, wash, and get to bed, and in the morning an extra thirty minutes makes it feel like you're already behind schedule.

- If booking B&Bs or hotels, check that there is somewhere safe and secure to put your bikes overnight. Youth Hostels are usually bike friendly and (at the time of writing), *Premier Inn* and *Travelodge* have always allowed us to keep bikes in our rooms. Other accommodations may offer similar facilities.

18.3 The Pros and Cons of a Support Crew

Even if you devise your own route, you may still want to get someone to come along to act as support crew.

There are a number of pros and cons to this, for both sides, so it's worth considering these beforehand.

Pros:

- Less to carry on the bike – if you have a car, van or motorhome following you, firstly, you'll be able to be a little more generous with what you take (you may, for example, pop in a spare wheel just in case) and secondly, you'll have a lot less to carry on the bike, making it much lighter and the going easier.

- Food and water supplies – depending on the level of support you want (and the support crew wish to offer), you can regularly get topped up with fresh stocks of food and water throughout the day. Doing this can help to keep overall spend on food and drink down for the journey, as it's generally cheaper to buy from a supermarket than cafes and pubs.

- Mechanical support – you may have someone with you who knows about repairing and maintaining bikes which, if you're not mechanically minded, is a huge plus. It's also possible to take tools in the supporting car – like a stand, or a full-sized track pump – which you won't be able to carry on the bike.

- Emotional support – having someone with you every step of the way can be a big help psychologically. If you're feeling low halfway through a day, some words of encouragement and some company can go a long way to getting your head back in the game.

- A chance for everyone to be involved – some people may not consider themselves fit or able to take on the challenge, but by being involved they still get to feel a part of it and experience the sights along the way. It also means that you can turn it into a family holiday, as long as everyone is happy with the arrangement. You could, for instance, spend the morning cycling, then see the sights as a family in the afternoon.

- If you're lucky enough to have your own camper van, it's certainly cheaper than hotels, and can offer a place to keep warm and dry on breaks, if the weather isn't in your favour.

- Equally, if you're camping, your support crew can go on ahead and get things set up for the evening, preparing meals and saving you from chores when you're tired after a long day on the bike. Be sure, though, that they realise what they're signing up for (see below)!

Cons

- Your crew will need to be able to put up with you when you're tired and maybe a little mardy. Fatigue leads to raw emotions, so you'll need to be good at getting along when the going gets tough.

- It's potentially hard work for the support crew. The days can be long and repetitive, and feel much less of an adventure. Daily supermarket trips and putting up and taking down tents everyday can get quite wearing.
- More people can mean more expense – there are more mouths to feed and more people to put up in accommodation.
- No instant access to your things. As described in our 'Coatgate' incident, not carrying all your own supplies can cause issues if you want or need something quickly.

18.4 Training

As everyone's needs are different, I haven't attempted to provide a day-by-day training plan. As a personal trainer of nearly 20 years, I know that everyone taking on this challenge will have different training requirements, so there can be no 'one-size-fits-all' training programme. Instead, I've provided a few key tips for making sure you get to the start in shape, well-prepared to take on your challenge.

Train

I know this might sound ridiculous, but I'm always

flabbergasted by the amount of people I meet, who take on a challenge having done little or no training. I once met a woman on a train, on the way to the starting line of the London Marathon. She seemed apprehensive, asking me lots of questions about what I'd done in preparation. She explained that she'd done a couple of runs of up to 6 miles – and asked me for reassurance that she'd be OK. I wanted to tell her that she should get off at the next stop for fear of hurting herself, or being carted off in an ambulance. I didn't of course. I think I said something along the lines of, 'start steady and just give it your best shot.' The thing is you can't really give an event your best shot without doing the training. It gets you both physically and mentally ready for what you're taking on – and both aspects are important, especially on longer challenges. It also means you're far less likely to come to harm. Anything is better than nothing, so even a few shorter rides in the week and a longer one at the weekend, building up over a number of weeks, will make a substantial difference.

Gradually Build Up the Mileage

It's commonplace these days to enter big events. Many people do not exercise at all, then attempt to get fit for a big challenge in around 12 weeks. It can be done, but the risks of injury are high as you have to increase the volume and intensity of training you are doing very quickly. Even if you are planning to do the End-to-End in a year's time, start doing something now. It doesn't need to be a huge excursion, or mean riding every day, but a couple of rides a week will stand you in good stead for when you do have to start ramping it up.

Once into training proper, only ever increase your ride distance by around ten per cent each time. That's not as much as it sounds. Doing a 60-mile ride one week would mean 66 miles the next. This approach allows your body time to adapt and decreases the likelihood of injury – especially to tendons and ligaments where there is less blood supply and recovery times are slower as a result.

Use the 'Cha-cha-cha' Rule

You can follow my 'cha-cha-cha' rule of training (I can't dance, but it's a good way of remembering it). Increase your distance for three weeks in a row, before easing it back in the fourth week, and then building up again for the next three weeks, and so on. Three steps forwards, one back, and repeat. This, again, is a great way of reducing the risk of overtraining and injury, allowing time for adaptation to occur.

Identify Your Weak Spots and Work on Them

If you know you have an achy lower back or tight shoulders, I can guarantee they'll be problem spots on a ride like this. You'll be on the move for hours each day, fixed in one position over the handlebars, repeating the same pedalling action time after time. This will place a lot of stress on your body so, if you have existing issues, it's much more likely they'll flare-up. Here are some common problem areas:

- Calves and Achilles – the pedalling action can make your lower legs very tight, so it's well worth stretching and strengthening them regularly.
- Hips – unlike when walking or running, you never fully extend your hips on a bike, so your glutes (bum) can become weakened and your hip flexors (at the front) can get very tight.
- Lower back – being bent over the handlebars all day puts a large amount of stress on your lower back. People think it makes it tight, but it's actually in a stretched position and so can become long and weak, requiring strengthening. Strangely, it will still feel tight because your body's natural reaction is to tense a muscle that has become overly lengthened, in an attempt to take it back to the correct length.
- Upper back and shoulders – again, being folded over the handlebars places a good deal of stress on these muscles. They can often be more uncomfortable than your legs on long rides.
- Hamstrings – the big muscles in your legs

obviously do a lot of work and can get tight or achy, in particular your hamstrings as they never fully lengthen whilst riding.

You should do stretching/mobility exercises at least two or three times each week, and the same for strengthening exercises. I use a foam roller to loosen any tight spots before I get out on a ride, and then I stretch after the ride. You should try to do mobility exercises as often as possible, even if not riding – doing them daily will definitely help.

I'll perform strengthening exercises in separate sessions to my cycling, unless I'm using my turbo trainer for a short workout of 30 minutes or less, in which case I'll do them straight afterwards. I vary the repetitions and weights used. Sometimes I'll do bodyweight or light weights for 15-25 repetitions, to help develop endurance in my muscles. At other times I'll use heavy weights, for 8 repetitions or less, to build strength. Both methods are needed in preparation for rides like Land's End to John o' Groats. The requirement for endurance is obvious, but strength and power are also essential to get you up those steeper hills, or when trying to maintain a decent pace (especially into a headwind).

You can find a range of stretching, mobility, and strengthening exercise routines helpful for cyclists, on my website: www.balancehealthandfitness.co.uk.

Focus on the Long One

Above everything else, getting some mileage under your belt is key to making your challenge achievable (and enjoyable). My target for any event like this is to ride the average distance we will be covering on two days in a row, and at least half of it on the third day. So, for example, if you're aiming for 80 miles a day, you'd do 80-80-40. Bank Holiday weekends are the perfect opportunity to do this. Try to pick somewhere that offers terrain that is similar to your route too - perfect practice makes perfect.

There are a number of reasons for this training target. Firstly, it gets you used to being on the bike with tired legs, something that is inevitable. Secondly, it's enough to get you fit without overdoing it and starting the ride exhausted. You may feel you need to do more than this and that's OK, you know your body best. My experience with multi-day rides is that I tend to get fitter as the ride goes on. The early days of the challenge give me stamina for what lies ahead, as long as I don't overdo it from the outset.

Taper

You should aim to reach peak fitness around 2-3 weeks before setting off on your ride then, in this final period, gradually taper (ease back) your exercise – initially to around 75 per cent of total volume, then 50 per cent (or even less) in the seven days leading up to the start. When and how much to taper is unique to you, and it is something you get a feel for as you take part in more events. During your taper, eat and drink normally.

In days gone by, the technique of carb-loading encouraged restricting carbohydrates seven days out from an event, then switching to carb-heavy meals four days before the start. The thought was that by cutting back carb intake, you 'hyper-tuned' your body to store them, and so when you increased consumption again in the days before the event, you would be able to begin with your energy stores at maximum capacity. This approach is now largely discouraged. Instead, it is suggested that you simply eat normally in the week before your event, whilst also easing back on training. This will help ensure that your muscles are fresh and energised when you set off.

Again, I must stress that when it comes to exercise, everybody is different. Some people prefer to keep doing some speedier sessions to make sure they feel sharp, whilst others like to just do very easy workouts to ensure they feel limber. Many don't like to rest, as they feel it makes them tight and sluggish. Personally, I take it very easy in the final phase, doing very gentle sessions, walks and stretching – this works for me. Listen to your body and just be sure not to overdo it. It's better to start your adventure slightly underdone than already burnt out.

18.5 Nutrition

Many, many books have been written on this subject so my intention here is not to deluge you with information. I certainly won't be delving into the mathematics of calories or counting your macros (the shortened term for the macronutrients – carbohydrates, fats, and proteins). Instead, here are what I consider to be the most important nutritional aspects to focus on.

Train Your Nutrition Too

Getting your eating and drinking strategy in place starts during your training. It's very risky to try new foods and drinks during the event, as you won't know how your body (in particular, your digestive system) will react. You don't want to be making emergency stops every time you see some bushes – you can easily get dehydrated, you won't enjoy it, and you won't be pleasant to ride with. Try different eating and drinking strategies on your longer training rides to find what works best for you.

Have Various Food and Drink Options to Hand

I try to have different types of fuel with me on longer rides, so that I always have what I need at any given time. I'll have a couple of water bottles, one with pure water and the other with some form of sports drink – or water and a sports drink combined. For food, I'll have something for fast-acting energy should I 'bonk' (the cycling term for a blood-sugar crash), an energy gel for example. I'll also have small snacks, like bananas or energy bars, and something a little stodgier to fill my stomach when I'm hungry. A sandwich or malt loaf, for example.

Don't Always Opt for Sugar

Yes, you'll need energy for all those miles, but you can get pretty sick of sweet stuff. If you always choose high-glycaemic index options (foods that cause a quick spike in blood-sugar levels) like chocolate, biscuits, or cake, you may find your energy levels soar briefly, but then dip dramatically. As I've grown older, I've found that I respond much better to savoury snacks and lunches. You'll often find you can eat a wider variety of foods on a bike ride than you could on something like a run, where the constant impact can trigger stomach issues. On this ride I found that fatty fry-ups kept me fuller and feeling better for longer than higher carbohydrate choices like porridge. It was also a great excuse to have a guilt-free fry-up every day. I'm not advocating this technique for everyone – it's certainly not the healthiest option and, of course, many people will have vegetarian or vegan diets.

Remember Your Nutrients

On a ride like this, getting enough energy will be your main focus, and it can mean you forget to eat healthier options, eschewing them in favour of high-calorie snacks. It's vital to keep some space for fruit and vegetables, though, as the vitamins, minerals, and antioxidants they contain help keep your immune system strong and prevent you getting run down. It's much less fun to ride with a cold, so try hard to get your five-a-day.

Be the Cow

Many people find long days of exercise mean they're not in the mood for food afterwards. This is a problem on a ride such as this, as you need to be refuelling regularly for the next day in the saddle. If you can't face a full meal, try grazing on snacks throughout the evening instead, or using liquid options like recovery drinks and protein shakes. Simon prefers this approach, whereas I'm absolutely starving after a long day's cycling. It may sound surprising, but you need to be careful not to over-eat. Due to tiredness and high exertion levels, it is possible to effectively 'panic eat' – overconsuming calories and putting weight on during multi-day events such as this.

Alcohol

I've decided not to dive too deep into the controversial realm of drinking on duty here. It certainly doesn't have performance-enhancing qualities (unless you're Simon), but it's entirely up to you how you approach it, and that will depend on the length and speed of your days, as well as your attitude to life and to the event. I tend to have very little, if any, during our multi-day rides, then I go mad afterwards and sometimes even have two beers. Simon, on the other hand, would fill one of his water-bottles with Stella or Kopparberg given half the chance – definitely don't do that.

18.6 Mental Coping Strategies

Cycling day after day, for hours on end, gives you a lot of time to think. Unfortunately, when you're not feeling so good, this can mean you get yourself into a bit of a pickle, so it's important to have coping strategies for when times are hard. Here are a few I've used with success over the years:

- *Chunking* – essentially this involves breaking longer days down into smaller parts. You can do this at a number of levels. Focus on riding until your next snack or meal break, that might be somewhere between 45 and 90 minutes of riding.

If you're not feeling good, you might want to break this down into even smaller sections, say 3-5 miles and, in really hard times, you might pick a spot in the distance to aim for, repeating this as you go along so that you're constantly achieving small victories. By using a variety of 'chunk sizes,' you'll regularly be hitting targets along the way. This will boost your motivation and make the day much more manageable.

- *Counting* – a very similar technique to 'chunking.' You might pick a number to count to, or a certain amount of time to ride for, convincing yourself that you'll just ride until that point, and then see how you feel. More often than not, you reach your number or time target and keep going. When things are really tough, I sometimes find myself aiming for just 20 – or sometimes only 10 more pedal turns – then again, and again, and so on until I get out of the dark spell.

- *Remember the training* – when you're doubting yourself, it's good to think back to all those miles you did in preparation (well, hopefully you did) as it can give you the confidence to know you can achieve your goal. Maybe even think of a ride that was truly horrific, but you made it through anyway. Getting things into perspective can help your situation seem a little better, at least long enough to get you through a tough patch.

- *Focus on the cause* – if you're raising money for charity, think of all the great things it will do. You can give yourself motivational reminders. Laminate a card with a photo or good luck message, tie it to your handlebars or tuck it in your pocket, so you can look at it when you need some visual or written encouragement. Get people to send messages of support via video, or social media, and watch/read these on your breaks. Anything that will help to spur you on is good.

- *Distract yourself* – sing a song (more than just the two-line song we managed), think of a problem you need to solve at work (yes, going to work in your head can actually be relaxing), or a DIY project that needs finishing. You can use just about anything that helps to take your mind off the pain and tiredness you're feeling.

- *Use relaxation techniques for pain relief* – one such method is to focus on the area that feels tight or uncomfortable. Take a big deep breath in and then, as you exhale, think about relaxing it. I'm amazed by how often this helps me to relax problem areas and ease the pain. Your mind is a truly powerful thing.

- *Enjoy it when the pain moves somewhere else* – this might sound a little counterintuitive, but pain in a different spot often feels good, if only because it's different. If your neck and shoulders have been feeling terrible and then, all of a sudden, it's your hips that start aching, it can feel like a relief – trust me!

- *Practice being bored* – whilst I said I never get bored on a ride, it's a good idea to train for the times where there is little or no mental stimulus. If you're on a particularly dull stretch of long road without much scenery to distract you, it's helpful to be good at going to other places, in your head. One of the (strange) ways I do this is through indoor training on the turbo trainer, or the Watt bike. Face it against a blank wall, then ride for a couple of hours or so – no music, no book to read, no input at all. It's as dull as dishwater, but it serves you well when you need it during your event.

- *Live in the present* – nature can be a really powerful aid. If you're struggling to get out of a negative mindset, focus all of your attention on what you can see, hear, smell, and taste as you are riding along. The view over the valley from the top of the hill, the buzzard gliding overhead, or the sound of the river roaring by. Bringing yourself back to living for the moment is a great way to start enjoying your ride again.

- *Shout out loud* – I find this technique useful if I'm in real pain, and there is some science to back it up. I remember seeing a study where people were asked to place their hand in a bucket of ice-cold water, and to see how long they could keep it in there. They had three options to help them – suffer in silence, scream out loud, or shout out a repertoire of obscenities. It was the Gordon Ramsay-style outburst which helped people to keep their hand in the bucket the longest. So, if you're reaching your endurance limit, let fly with some expletives or just scream. It really can help! Just make sure there are no families nearby at the time.

- *Train* – by getting outside for hours at a time, you'll develop your own coping mechanisms for when times are hard. Whether that's anticipating tucking into a big bowl of Spaghetti Bolognese followed by ice cream later that evening (works for me), imagining the faces of your supporters as they greet you at the finish-line, or something completely different doesn't matter, as long as it gets you through.

18.7 The Bike

It is possible to ride almost any type of pedal-propelled vehicle along the route – the End-to-End has been completed by bicycle, tricycle, unicycle, and penny farthing. Here are a few different bikes, and reasons why you might consider them:

- *Touring bikes* – often made from steel, they offer a

tough, durable frame and have plenty of attachment points for pannier bags – if going self-supported. You'll also get a choice of handlebar set-ups. Most touring bikes use the drop bars you see on road bikes, but some have flat bars like those found on mountain bikes. On the flipside, the steel frame will make them heavier, so they're not always the ideal choice if you feel the need, the need for speed!

- *Hybrid bikes* – as the name suggests, these combine elements of road, touring, and mountain bikes into an all-round package. On long days in the saddle, the upright position and wider tyres will be more comfortable for many. Swapping to bull horn handlebars (or buying add-on bull horns for straight bars) can provide versatility and comfort when it comes to grip. Hybrid bikes aren't necessarily slow, but the next option will likely be what you opt for if out-and-out speed is your goal.
- *Road bikes* – lighter and with a more aggressive set-up, these days the road bike is the choice of many who take on this challenge, especially if they have support crew transporting their gear for them. Recent years have seen a growth in the choice and popularity of bike bags that do not require panniers, so it is possible to use road bikes for a self-supported attempt. Just make sure your bike is compatible with the amount and type of

luggage. You get a choice of aluminium, carbon or even titanium frames, each with its own advantages. All these materials are strong (otherwise they wouldn't build bikes out of them), but good quality carbon is generally the lightest and therefore best for speed. I say "generally," because how much you and your kit weigh obviously impacts on speed too! Losing weight might have a bigger impact on overall speed than buying an expensive carbon bike. If you plan to include some off-road riding, make sure the frame and tyres are suitable for your needs.

- *Adventure bikes* – this style of bike is fairly new to the market and can be carbon or aluminium. Adventure bikes are purposely designed to be the 'do anything, go anywhere' bike. They have a more comfortable geometry than traditional road bikes and can fit much wider tyres, which vastly increases comfort, especially when off-road. If you were planning to use a lot of the gravel paths on the *Sustrans* network for your ride, for instance, this style of bike would be a grand choice. It's perfectly at home on the road too, so you can switch from one surface to the other at will.

Whatever bike you choose, get it early and practice on it. As I discovered, it can often seem hard going when you're getting used to a new style of bike, but the more you ride it, the easier it becomes. Many bike shops will let you take a bike for a test ride these days, so you can get a feel for it before forking out your hard-earned cash. Even lower end bikes aren't cheap, so it's definitely a wise move to try before you buy.

Tyres and Gears

It's also worth considering your choice of tyres and gears. Without getting too bogged down in technical stuff, wider tyres generally offer more comfort and more grip. More comfort because you can use them at lower pressures; more grip because the width means greater surface area on the road.

As well as width, you'll want to consider the suitability of the tyre for the terrain. You may want gravel tyres if you're going to mix up your route between road and some of the gravel trails which you'll find along sections of the *Sustrans'* routes. It's well worth discussing with your local bike shop which tyres will fit on your bike and best help to get you where you want to be, whilst keeping you upright and comfortable.

It's also worth talking to them about suitable gearing. You need your bike set up so you can find a gear to get up hills comfortably (often at the equivalent of walking speed), but also move quickly along flat and downhill sections – without pedalling at a million miles an hour. If you're a bike geek and you know all about gear inches, you'll already have formed opinions on what works best. If, however, you're thinking about purchasing a bike, or you're finding the training tough on your current ride, head to a bike shop and discuss your planned challenge with them. They'll be willing and able to set your bike up with the right drivetrain (all the bits that enable you to move the bike along) for your needs.

18.8 Clothing and Equipment

What you pack will depend on how you're doing it – self-supported or with a support team. Obviously, solo travellers will need to pack carefully in order to keep the weight down. That said, there are some fundamentals you'll need – whichever way you're doing it:

- *Cycling shorts* – I can't stress just what a difference these make. The right padding, in the right place, is essential for staying comfortable in the saddle. Once, on a group charity ride of 350 miles over four days – from London to Brussels – we met a gentleman taking part who was riding a new bike and not using cycling shorts. By the end of day one he was in severe discomfort and by that, I mean walking like a cross between John Wayne and a robot. That evening, he had to get a member of the support crew to take him to a bike shop to buy some shorts. I'd suggest taking two pairs so you can wash one pair while wearing the others – it'll play a big part in helping to keep saddle sore at bay.

- *Gloves* – the same gentleman also failed to wear cycling gloves and his hands suffered terribly as a result. On our 24-hour ride from London to Paris, even with plenty of cushioning in my gloves, I lost the use of a couple of fingers in each hand for well over a week afterwards. I was genuinely worried at one stage that I would never regain full use of them. That was a pretty extreme ride, being on the bike for so long in one go, but your hands will suffer a lot of vibration and impact on multi-day rides like this, so it can be a good idea to get the bike shop to fit your handlebars with extra-thick tape for added comfort. Don't forget some waterproof gloves too. Even in summertime, there's no guarantee you won't get cold and wet.

- *Cycling jerseys* – it's worthwhile having a couple of these, as wearing sweaty, smelly kit isn't pleasant. The pockets are really useful for storing snacks and tools for quick access. You could take a short-sleeved and long-sleeved, or just get a pair of removable arm warmers to wear early in the day, when it's still a little chilly.

- *Waterproof jacket* – I say "waterproof," but often the really high-quality waterproof jackets, like the highly-reflective ones you see commuters wear, are sealed, and therefore make you sweat a lot.

Don't be afraid to spend more for jackets that are light but more resistant to water – being wet makes you cold, and being cold makes you miserable. In my most recent event, I discovered the Gore Shakedry 1985 insulated jacket. It is truly amazing! It's lightweight, warm, and completely waterproof in the worst weather, yet you don't sweat at all. It's expensive, but worth every penny to stay warm and dry.

- *Helmet* – it's not a legal requirement, and it's an entirely personal choice, but I just don't think it's worth the risk not to wear one – cycling on Britain's roads can be dangerous! You'll never find me out on my bike without one. If you really can't face wearing one, check out the coats with inflatable collars which activate as you fall.

- *Layers* – on colder days, a jersey and a waterproof won't be enough, so long-sleeved sports base layers, tights, or arm and leg warmers, are good to have to hand. And I know it's not considered cool or fashionable, but bright, luminous kit is a very good idea, in particular if you intend to ride busy A-roads for much of the route. Be safe, be seen!

- *Lights* – you never know when you may be delayed and end up cycling in the dark. They add to your visibility during the day too. Even if you never turn them on, it's good to know they are there, and they can always be used as a torch for your campsite. If you're riding smaller roads, you'll need more powerful lights than the standard commuting option. Bear in mind that the batteries on USB-chargeable versions can run down pretty quickly, so have the portable charge pack that I mentioned earlier, to hand.

- *Cycling shoes and overshoes* – one of my biggest mistakes on this ride was not choosing to use clip-in pedals. Not just because they're more efficient but also because, with cycling shoes, you can wear the proper waterproof overshoes when it's hammering down – and not completely lose the feeling in your toes! If you're nervous about doing this, practice first on a soft grassy surface or, to be even safer, on a turbo trainer. I'd recommend opting for the mountain bike pedals that allow you to clip in on both sides. It's much easier than trying to kick the pedal around into the correct position whilst moving along.

- *Changeable glasses* – many cycling glasses come with changeable lenses – from clear lenses right through to darker ones for sunny days. These are incredibly useful – on wet windy days with poor light, using the clear visors is a great way to protect your eyes. You can then switch to sunglasses if and when you're lucky enough to need them!

- *Warmer clothes for the evenings* – it can get very chilly in the UK at night if you're camping. If you're staying in four-star hotels all the way, by all means just pack a pair of pants, flip flops and order room service.

In terms of equipment, take the following:

- *Spare inner tubes and a foldable spare tyre* – we were incredibly lucky to suffer only a few punctures but it's best to be prepared for the worst-case scenario. I'd suggest having at least three spare inner tubes to hand. You'll need to be very unfortunate to suffer three punctures in a day, but it has been known, especially if you don't check the inner wall of the tyre thoroughly for the cause of the initial flat. To be safe, take a puncture repair kit in case you run out of inner tubes, or get the sealant that you can spray into an inner tube through the valve. It's only a short-term fix, but it'll get you to your destination where you can carry out proper repairs. Similarly, you may consider taking tyre patches – effectively large sticking plasters – to use should a tyre wall get damaged. You can switch to tubeless tyres if your bike allows, and you know what you're doing with them.
- *A miniature pump* – you can get ones with pressure gauges, so you can be very precise about tyre pressures, but it isn't essential. A tyre that feels

firm but with a little bit of give in it will work fine for those of us not competing in professional Grand Tour races.

- *A list of bike shops on route* – this is just common sense and a good precaution. I would also highly recommend having your bike properly serviced, prior to setting off.
- *Tyre levers (or lever)* – I use a Crank Brothers' lever and it's awesome. It's a single, sturdy lever with some nifty features, as opposed to the traditional method of using two smaller ones. It makes it really easy to get the tyre off (and on again) when you need to change a flat.
- *A multi-tool* – one that fits all the nuts and bolts on your bike and allows you to make running (or rather, riding) repairs.
- *A bike bag (or bags)* – Again, this will depend on how you're doing the trip. If you have a support team, you may just need a small saddle bag for your spares. You might like to have a top tube bag for snacks too. If you're self-supported, you might have a range of bags. Alpkit, Altura and Ortlieb make good waterproof options, and you can buy dry bags to put inside to ensure your things stay that way. Those of you on touring or adventure bikes may use pannier bags. If so, just be careful to load the weight evenly – left to right and front to back. Practice riding with them loaded a

number of times before you set off.

- *Chamois cream* – preventing chaffing will be very high on your list of essential things to do. I've used Assos Chamois Crème and the wonderfully titled, Swerve Bum Cream, and been impressed by both of them. Famous round-the-world cyclist, Mark Beaumont, recommends Paw Paw cream, and I guess he should know what works!
- *Navigation kit* – if you're going 'old-skool' and just using paper maps, get a map case – to keep them protected from the elements. The more tech savvy of you might be using a GPS device or a smartphone. Either way, don't forget to take charging cables and the clasps that attach them to the bike (bring spare bands for these just in case). Again, unless you have support crew following you all the way, a portable battery charger is a must, and I'd take one even if I were being supported. I'd also take a paper map as back-up, should technology let you down.
- *An emergency spoke* – this is a great piece of kit. Essentially, it's a temporary spoke, made of strong cord, that you can fit in place should one break. It'll keep your wheel safer and stronger, until you can get to a bike shop for a proper replacement.
- *Chain lubricant* – a small bottle, just to keep things running smoothly. Muc Off, ProGold or Fenwick's are all good choices.

- *A good bike lock* (or two) – if you are riding self-supported, particularly, you'll want a light lock. I use a Kryptonite Kryptoflex cable, combined with a D-Lock, to ensure I can secure the whole bike – wheels and all. Also, don't forget to take bags and GPS devices off overnight, for peace of mind.
- *Suntan lotion, after sun, and insect repellent* – to keep you protected from the elements and the bugs.

I can't emphasise enough how important it is to get your set-up right before you start. If in doubt, pay for a professional bike-fit to minimise your risk of saddle sores, and other aches and pains. You won't regret a single penny three days into your ride, believe me. You might also want to try a few different saddles until you find the one best suited to your needs. Search for local bike retailers that offer fit services and contact them with your questions.

18.9 Tips to Make Your Days Run Smoothly

Here are a few final tips to ensure days run efficiently and to time (something I was very bad at in the beginning, and that I've worked hard to improve over the years):

- *Set a start time for each day* – this will stop you getting into the habit of sleeping in, starting late, and finishing late. As tiredness sets in on rides like this, it's easy to allow a sort of malaise to set in, limiting your time for effective refuelling and recovery, and making you feel even worse on the bike the next day.

- *Have a route back-up* – if your GPS decides to play up or dies, it's good to have the route stored on your phone, or to have a paper map to hand. Personally, I'll always have one non-digital option to fall back on, just in case.
- *Study the map* – have a good idea of where you're heading each day, in case you have to take diversions due to road closures or other unexpected occurrences.
- *Pack the things you'll need most often on the top* – whether bike-packing or for a support vehicle, it's very frustrating when you can't find what you need when you need it. Always put things back in exactly the same place, so that you know where to look for them. You'll be amazed just how much kit you have. Without organisation the inside of cars and camper vans soon begin to look like the aftermath of a force 5 hurricane.
- *Carry out quick daily checks on your bike before setting off* – are the tyre pressures OK? How are the tyres looking – any tears or debris stuck in them? Are your brakes working well? Is there enough lubricant on the chain? Any loose parts? It'll only

take five or ten minutes, but it could save you hours if it prevents something going wrong.

18.10 Most Important of All

Hopefully, some of this information will prove useful in helping you on your End-to-End adventure, or any ride of a similar nature. Everyone will get there a slightly different way: whether that's using a different route, speed, type of bike; or even doing it in small chunks over a number of weeks, months, or years, rather than all in one go.

It doesn't matter how you get there, or how long it takes you, only that you do it. Most importantly, don't forget to enjoy it.

'Hae a guid journey!' or 'Vyaj salow!'.

That's the Scots, and Cornish for: 'Have a good journey!'

Acknowledgements

Firstly, I must thank the End-to-End adventure team from all those years ago. A huge thank you to Bek and Kirsty for being our support crew and for putting up with our behaviour and demands for nearly a fortnight and 1,000 miles. Thank you to Simon for being a great training partner and friend. You are like a brother to me.

My thanks to Rob for joining us on those final few days. And thank you to our fabulous friends who came to Cornwall to cheer us over the line and celebrate our achievement. It was a weekend I will never forget.

To the present, thank you to my partner Lou for your endless support and encouragement and for making me believe I could be a writer. I love all of our adventures. I can't wait to write about them in future books and look forward to our next one.

Thank you also to my parents, Bill and Jude, and my sister Suzi and her family for showing me endless love and support. Thank you for always supporting the decisions I make. And for helping me to live my dreams.

There are many of you to thank for assisting me in getting this book written and published. Thank you again to Lou, my parents, and Lou's mum Heather for your proof-reading and suggestions and to Simon for letting me tell our story. Thank you to Simon Toseland for your eagle-eyed editing and for helping me bring the story and the characters to life on the page. My thanks to Catherine Clarke for your beautiful, vibrant cover design. You are truly talented. Huge thanks also to Katharine Smith for your skilled work formatting the book interior and helping to make it look better than I could ever have hoped.

And finally, my thanks to all of you for reading it. A huge thank you to all of you who have followed and supported me and my business, Balance Health and Fitness, over the years. I hope in some way that I have helped you to feel fitter, healthier, and happier. If so, then I am delighted.

One final cheeky thank you in advance to those of you who enjoyed reading this book. Thank you for being so kind as to write a lovely review for it on Amazon or wherever you bought it from, for telling your friends and family about it, or better still, for buying them a copy too!

About the Author

Paul Waters is a fitness professional and adventurer. He has worked in the health and fitness industry for nearly 20 years. Apart from three weeks as a barman in a bingo hall while studying at university, it is all he has ever done. He is the owner of Balance Health and Fitness, spending his days writing or teaching about wellbeing or working with individuals and companies to help people get fitter, healthier, happier, and stay that way.

Since 2005, he has run numerous marathons and one very painful ultra-marathon. After cycling from John o' Groats to Land's End in 2007 with his good friend Simon, he has taken on numerous challenges on two wheels, including:

- riding nearly 300 miles from London to Paris in 24 hours
- scaling Britain's famous Three Peaks and cycling the 450-mile distance between them over four days, and
- conquering the three ascents of the infamous Mont Ventoux in a single day.

Most recently, he cycled over 2,000 miles around Britain for charity with his partner Lou in an attempt to pedal through every National Park and Area of Outstanding Natural Beauty on the mainland, becoming a member of the Cape Wrath Fellowship along the way.

He lives just outside of Bristol with Lou and their two cats, Basil and Mog. Together, they enjoy tending to their allotment, spending time in nature, and eating Lou's delicious homemade baking.

www.balancehealthandfitness.co.uk

www.facebook.com/BalanceHealthFitness

Bibliography

Bill Bryson, The Road to Little Dribbling: More Notes from a Small Island, London: Black Swan, 2016.

Bristol Post. This is why pirates talk with a Bristolina accent on Talk Like a Pirate Day, by Lewis Pennock. https://www.bristolpost.co.uk/news/history/pirates-talk-bristol-accent-1049915.
January 14th, 2018, updated September 19th, 2019.

Culture Trip. Inside Bristol's Fascinating Pirate Past. https://theculturetrip.com/europe/united-kingdom/articles/inside-bristols-fascinating-pirate-past/, by Hannah Wakefield, written in association with Epigram, a student publication at the University of Bristol.
April 10th, 2018.

Encyclopaedia Britannica. Robin Hood: Legendary Hero.
https://www.britannica.com/topic/Robin-Hood.
2020.

Forces War Records. Unit History: Commando Training Centre.
https://www.forces-war-records.co.uk/units/1362/commando-training-centre/.
2008-2020.

Historic England. Listing.
https://historicengland.org.uk/listing/.
2020.

History.com. Loch Ness Monster.
https://www.history.com/topics/folklore/loch-ness-monster.
June 10th, 2019.

Landmark Trust. The marisco Years: Lundy under Norman Rule.
https://www.landmarktrust.org.uk/lundyisland/discovering-lundy/history/the-mariscos1/.
2020.

Mail Online. Weatherman (with a dry sense of humour) puts his own village of Wetwang on the map, by Chris Brooke. https://www.dailymail.co.uk/news/article-1212923/Weatherman-Paul-Hudson-puts-village-Wetwang-map.html.
September 12th, 2009.

Nottinghamshire County Council. History of Sherwood Forest, Robin Hood and Major Oak.
https://www.nottinghamshire.gov.uk/culture-leisure/country-parks/sherwood-forest/history-of-sherwood-forest-robin-hood-and-major-oak.
2020.

Office for National Statistics. Population estimates for the UK, England and Wales, Scotland and Northern Ireland, provisional, mid-2019.
https://www.ons.gov.uk/peoplepopulationandcommunity/populationandmigration/populationestimates/bulletins/annualmidyearpopulationestimates/mid2019.
May 6th, 2020.

RAC. RAC Route Planner.
https://www.rac.co.uk/route-planner/.
2019.

Scotland Info Guide. The Caledonian Canal.
https://www.scotlandinfo.eu/caledonian-canal/.
2019.

Scots Index. Scotland's Land Mass.
http://www.scotsindex.org/scotlands-land-mass/.
2013.

The Vintage News. The popular "pirate accent" is based on Robert newton's perrformance in the movie "Treasure Island", by Domagoj Valijak.
https://www.thevintagenews.com/2018/02/20/pirate-accent/.
February 20th, 2018.

Visit Inverness & Loch Ness. The Highland Midge: How to avoid midges in the Scottish Highlands.
https://www.visitinvernesslochness.com/blog/the-highland-midge/.
May 9th, 2018.

Visit John o' Groats. A Brief History of John o' Groats.
https://www.visitjohnogroats.com/information/history-john-ogroats/.
2019.

Wikipedia. Land's End to John o' Groats.
https://en.wikipedia.org/wiki/Land%27s_End_to_John_o%27_Groats.
October, 2015.

Wikipedia. Wikipedia: List of hoaxes on Wikipedia.
https://en.wikipedia.org/wiki/Wikipedia:List_of_hoaxes_on_Wikipedia.
May 27th, 2020.

ZME Science. Study shows Wikipedia accuracy is 99.5%, by Mihai Andrei.
https://www.zmescience.com/science/study-wikipedia-25092014/.
February 22nd, 2019.

9 781838 432904